Management Extra

BUSINESS ENVIRONMENT

ELSEVIER

eLEARN

Pergamon
Flexible
Learning

AMSTERDAM • BOSTON • HEIDELBERG • LONDON • NEW YORK • OXFORD • PARIS •
SAN DIEGO • SAN FRANCISCO • SINGAPORE • SYDNEY • TOKYO

Elsevier Butterworth-Heinemann
Linacre House, Jordan Hill, Oxford OX2 8DP
30 Corporate Drive, Burlington, MA 01803

First published 2005

© 2005 Wordwide Learning Limited adapted by Elearn Limited
Published by Elsevier Ltd
All rights reserved

Permissions may be sought directly from Elsevier's Science & Technology
Rights Department in Oxford, UK: phone: (+44) 1865 843830, fax: (+44)
1865 853333, e-mail: permissions@elsevier.co.uk. You may also complete
your request on-line via the Elsevier homepage (www.elsevier.com), by
selecting 'Customer Support' and then 'Obtaining Permissions'

British Library Cataloguing in Publication Data
A catalogue record for this book is available from the British Library

Library of Congress Cataloguing in Publication Data
A catalogue record for this book is available from the Library of Congress

ISBN 0 7506 6679 X

For information on all Elsevier Butterworth-Heinemann publications
visit our website at www.books.elsevier.com

Printed and bound in Italy

Management Extra

BUSINESS ENVIRONMENT

Contents

Activities

Figures

Tables

Series preface

*'I hear I forget
I see I remember
I do I understand'*

Galileo

Management Extra is designed to help you put ideas into practice. Each book in the series is full of thought-provoking ideas, examples and theories to help you understand the key management concepts of our time. There are also activities to help you see how the concepts work in practice.

The text and activities are organised into bite-sized themes or topics. You may want to review a theme at a time, concentrate on gaining understanding through the text or focus on the activities whilst dipping into the text for reference.

The activities are varied. Some are work-based, asking you to consider changing, developing and extending your current practice. Others ask you to reflect on new ideas, check your understanding or assess the application of concepts in different contexts. The activities will give you a valuable opportunity to practise various techniques in a safe environment.

And, finally, exploring and sharing your ideas with others can be very valuable in making the most of this resource.

More information on using this book as part of a course or programme of learning is available on the Management Extra website.

www.managementextra.co.uk

Uncover the challenges facing your organisation

Do you know what your organisation is working to achieve? Can you explain its key goals? Do you understand the reasons for its major priorities? Do you know what challenges it is facing?

The big picture

To answer these questions you need to take a strategic view of your business. You are likely to contribute to the process of developing and implementing strategy, even if in an indirect way. You will be more able to fulfil your responsibilities if you have an understanding of the broad picture in which your organisation operates.

This book looks at how your organisation works and at the major factors that influence it. By developing your awareness of your organisation you will be able to contribute more effectively to achieving the overall goals.

Your objectives are to:

◆ Explore the nature of your organisation

◆ Assess the impact of internal factors such as culture and structure on organisations

◆ Conduct an internal environment analysis

◆ Identify stakeholders and their impact on the business

◆ Evaluate trends in the external environment that will affect organisations in the future

◆ Explore your organisation's position in the marketplace

◆ Use analytical techniques to uncover the opportunities and threats to your business.

1 The organisation in context

Business environment is about exploring the nature of the organisation you are working in. This first theme considers a number of fundamental questions about the organisation: What's the organisation for? What major factors influence organisations? Why are there different types of organisation? What is your organisation's vision for the future? And how is the vision translated into a strategy for every level?

Think of this big picture as a fly-past in an aeroplane at altitude before the detailed plotting of the landmarks and features of your business.

Within this theme you will:

◆ Review the core components of your organisation and what makes it different from others

◆ Identify ways to communicate the goals of an organisation

◆ Identify your organisation's vision, mission and values and how these translate into strategic objectives

◆ Develop a strategic understanding of your business.

> 'Perception is strong and sight weak. In strategy it is important to see distant things as if they were close and to take a distanced view of close things.'
> **Miyamoto Musashi (1584–1645)**

The nature of organisations

A simple way of looking at what an organisation is and what it is for is to picture the core of the organisation as a system that transforms inputs into outputs that are provided to customers. See Figure 1.1.

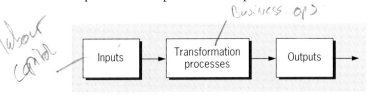

Figure 1.1 *A basic transformation process*

◆ Inputs include labour, raw materials, expertise, capital, data and information

◆ Transformation processes include business operations and production processes

◆ Outputs include goods, services, profits and wages, and information and waste products.

Transformation processes may involve converting inputs, transporting, combining or adding value to them in some other way in order to produce outputs that customers want.

This system for transforming inputs into outputs does not exist in a vacuum. It is not isolated from the environment in which it operates. On the contrary, the system exists in a unique context and it interacts with factors in this context in a dynamic way – constantly influencing and being influenced by them. For a start, the system provides its outputs to customers outside the system, and if there are no customers then the system is unlikely to continue to operate for long.

This suggests that the organisation can be seen as an 'open' system – the effectiveness and efficiency of the basic system are affected by major factors in the context in which the organisation operates.

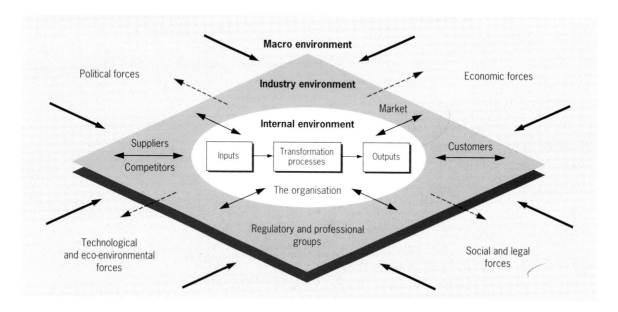

Figure 1.2 *The context in which the organisation works*

The internal environment

This includes the system (inputs, transformation processes and outputs) and all of the resources, knowledge and the actions of decision makers and employees that make up the organisation. All these factors may be controlled and deployed to enable the system to operate effectively and efficiently. The organisation as a whole has most control over its internal environment; it can shape its strategy and organise and direct its resources to achieve what it wants to achieve.

The industry environment

This is the external environment closest to the organisation. It is the organisation's marketplace, where it buys its materials, resources and other inputs and provides goods and services to customers. It also includes competitors, those organisations that compete for the same customers. The industry environment affects the organisation's scope for action, but the organisation can also take action to influence the industry environment. For example, it may develop partnerships with suppliers or enter into a price war with competitors. In some industries it is also vital to influence standards and regulations and the more aggressive organisations also set out to change the structure of their industry and the way in which the competitive game is played.

The macro environment

This is the 'playing field' for all businesses in the global and national economy. It is the external environment that provides a general background in which all organisations operate. It is made up of political, economic, social, technological, legal and eco-environmental forces. These act on organisations and their industry environments. For example, legislation affects an organisation's ability to hire and fire, merge with other organisations and dispose of its waste products. The organisation cannot control these forces, and it may not be able to influence them. However, much of the lobbying of political parties and governments by organisations is aimed at influencing these macro forces.

The following brief example shows how the system of inputs, transformation processes and outputs interacts with its internal and external environments.

Marks & Spencer plc, the UK-based retailer, uses its shops, staff, supplies and capital (inputs) to deliver (transformation processes) food, clothing, homeware and financial services (outputs) to its customers (industry environment). Poor performance in its market sector (industry environment) has led to changes in product design, business relations and corporate strategy (internal environment). A decision to close 18 shops in France in March 2001 brought the threat of legal action from the French Prime Minister, Lionel Jospin, over lack of consultation with store staff (macro environment).

Different strokes for...

It soon becomes apparent why there are so many different types of organisation. Each has different inputs, transformation processes and outputs, and operates in different industry environments.

Consider the examples in Table 1.1.

Organisation	Inputs	Transformation processes	Outputs	Internal environment	Industry environment
UK farming	Seeds, animals, farms, farmhands, machines	Milking, tending, harvesting	Milk, meat, cereals, eggs	Family owned, tight finance, subsidised	Disease, supermarket control, organic and genetic food
Microsoft plc	Code, data, IT skills, reinvesting, high-tech facilities	Programming, Web development	Software, MSN (Web portal)	Democratic culture, fast changing, high spending	Legal threats, tech market decline, intense competition
The Roman Catholic Church	Clergy, churches, parishioners, scripture	The Mass, fasting, praying, loving neighbour	Salvation, grace, goodness, collections	Bureaucratic, slow changing, same product, funded by members	Shortage of employees, materialism
The UK Government	Budget, ministers, Parliament	Consultation, law making, spending	Law, policy, information, taxes	Democratic, traditional, public funding	Lobbyists, the people, markets, disasters

Table 1.1 *The influence of operating context on organisations*

Why analyse the organisation's environment?

Environmental influences have implications for the organisation's direction and strategy.

You analyse your organisation's environment in order to make decisions and take action. If you can analyse the organisation you are part of and the major factors that are likely to impact on performance, then you can begin to understand and make plans, albeit for an uncertain future. Everyone, whatever their level in the organisation, should be involved because strategy cascades to all parts of an organisation. You will make better decisions at your level if you understand how your organisation works in its environment and how your area fits into this, and you will contribute to more informed decision making. This book will enable you to make decisions based on your business awareness. Business awareness is not an end in itself.

A good example of the sort of environmental impacts that businesses have to contend with is that of the recent 'mad cow' disease in the UK. Farmers were working within the regulations and competing with other farmers in producing beef, milk and dairy products. But one unexpected microbe and they all had to abide by regulations that required herds to be decimated. Farmers engaged in plenty of lobbying to have the regulations softened, but all of these failed. The major threat, from the farmers' view, was from the government and the external environment. Other organisations, such as the McDonald's hamburger chain, supermarkets and restaurants, all had their own way of dealing with this national event but the impact was felt nevertheless. This issue demonstrates that the impacts rippled across from the external environment to the operation of individual internal company processes.

How to analyse the business environment

So, how do you go about analysing your environment? The answer is to use a variety of environmental analysis tools to help you. The tools you will use as you work through this book are as follows:

◆ The balanced scorecard
◆ Portfolio analysis
◆ Stakeholder analysis
◆ Market research
◆ Ansoff's matrix
◆ Porter's Five Force model
◆ Benchmarking
◆ PESTLE analysis
◆ SWOT analysis.

Change and the organisation

> Increasing competition in the banking sector has led UK banks to operate a merger and acquisition strategy to stay ahead. Royal Bank of Scotland took over NatWest in 2000 despite initial opposition, but the City liked the look of its first full-year results (March 2001): revenue growth of 12%, cost growth of just 1% and over 30% growth in profits.

Change is the catalyst for environmental analysis. It is why we must analyse and analyse again. Because of the rapid, ever-changing nature of the environment, the impacts you face are changing. If you are complacent, you and your organisation can be caught out.

It is when organisations are moving along smoothly – in a state of equilibrium – that they should start to worry, according to complexity or chaos theory. How many of the 43 quality companies mentioned in Tom Peters' *In Search of Excellence* (1982) are still doing well? Five at the last count.

Activity 1
Focus on your organisation

Objective

Use this activity to identify the key components of your organisation.

The system that transforms inputs into outputs in your organisation operates in a unique context and interacts with the factors in this context in a dynamic way. This suggests that the organisation can be seen as an 'open' system – the effectiveness and efficiency of the basic system are affected by major factors in the context in which the organisation operates.

Task

The key components of the organisation as an open system are listed in the chart below. Give examples of these components for your organisation.

Inputs

Transformation processes

Outputs

Internal environment

Industry environment

Feedback

This activity should help you to get to grips with the nature of your organisation. Check back to Table 1.1 to make sure your examples of components are appropriate. You may want to compare your responses with colleagues. You could also identify the components that make up your unit or department. How do these compare with the components you have identified for your organisation?

The strategy process

Strategy is concerned with the long-term direction of the organisation. It determines the scope and focus of the organisation's activities. Strategies can make organisations great or bring them down.

Eastman Kodak dominated the photographic market until the late 1970s/early 1980s. Then, due to competition from Fuji, failure of its own product launches and the arrival of the Japanese 35mm camera, it had to have a strategic rethink. The company decided to focus its initiatives in two main areas: imaging and life sciences. Digital imaging in particular has enabled Kodak to strike back at the competition. There have been difficulties along the way, and more tactical and strategic rethinks have been necessary, but Kodak is still a strong brand and seems to keep coming back every time it is written off.

Source: *Grant and Neupert* (1999)

As the example of Eastman Kodak shows, forming strategy is not just a one-off exercise. In a changing environment, it's a continual process. The strategy process involves asking the key questions shown in Figure 1.3.

> **Strategy is about how to get from where you are now to where you want to be.**

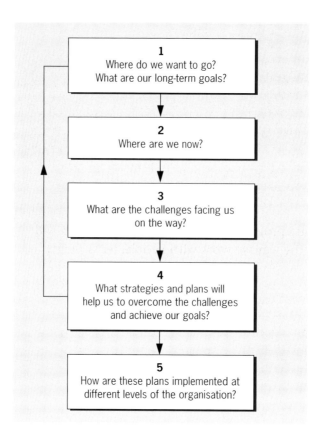

Figure 1.3 *The strategy process*

To answer these questions you can go through a number of stages:

1 Define the purpose of the organisation, what we want to achieve, and the values that will guide our actions and our long-term goals.

2 Analyse the environments that the organisation is operating in. These include the organisation's internal environment and the factors in the external environment that affect the organisation.

3 Identify opportunities and threats in the external environment, and strengths and weaknesses in the organisation.

4 Devise plans for achieving your goals that make the most of opportunities, counter threats, improve on internal strengths and overcome weaknesses.

5 Cascade plans throughout the organisation so that every level of the organisation contributes to achieving the long-term goals.

Purpose

A starting point for strategy is to have a vision for the future. This is a wish statement or a dream designed to inspire. Then there needs to be a clear purpose and goals. This hardens up the dream. These may be stated in a mission statement. Mission statements define the core business of the organisation – what it is and what it isn't. They should also communicate the priorities of the organisation and set out the direction in which the organisation is heading.

Here are some examples of mission statements:

BP Group's mission statement:
The world's need for energy is growing steadily day by day. Energy and materials, used safely and efficiently, are essential to the prosperity and growth of every country and every region in the world. Sustaining and enhancing our quality of life depends on them. Our goal is to play a leading role in meeting these needs from oil, gas, solar power and petrochemicals without damaging the environment.

Ours is a positive and progressive involvement. Innovation will be the hallmark of the way we work with people, technology, assets and relationships. We will always be constructive, using our know-how to produce constructive and creative solutions to every challenge.

Our success depends on our making, and being seen to make, a distinctive contribution to every activity in which we are involved.

Source: *BP* (www)

Harley-Davidson's mission statement:
We fulfill dreams through the experiences of motorcycling – by providing to motorcyclists and to the general public an expanding line of motorcycles, branded products and services in selected market segments.

Source: *Harley-Davidson* (www)

Pfizer, a leading pharmaceutical company, reported on its website in 2001:

Our mission: We will become the world's most valued company to patients, customers, colleagues, investors, business partners and the community where we work and live.

Our purpose: We dedicate ourselves to humanity's quest for longer, healthier, happier lives through innovation in pharmaceutical, consumer, and animal health products.

Source: *Pfizer* (www)

Some organisations do not set out a mission in a clear statement. This may be because the organisation is large and diverse and it is difficult to make a short summary of the organisation's purpose that is meaningful to everyone. Capturing the distinguishing features of the organisation, those that set it apart from its competitors, is key to producing a memorable mission statement.

However, even if an organisation does not identify its mission in a clear statement, it is often possible to gain a sense of an organisation's purpose and main goals by looking at its annual reports or at the corporate information section of its website.

Here are some examples:

Tesco, the leading UK supermarket retailer, says its aim is: Growing the business to create value for customers to earn their lifetime loyalty.

Source: *Tesco* (www)

Vodafone, a leading mobile telecommunications network provider, says:

Vodafone aims to be the world's leading wireless telecommunications and information provider, generating more customers, more services and more value than any of its competitors.

Source: *Vodafone* (www)

On **Exxon Mobil's** website in 2004, CEO Lee R Raymond wrote:

Exxon Mobile is committed to being the world's premier petroleum and petrochemical company.

Source: *Exxon Mobil* (www)

Values

While a mission is about the purpose and overall goals, a set of values can give the organisation its guiding principles that govern the way it will act. Many organisations communicate their values. For example:

Royal Dutch/Shell explores its general business principles under nine main headings: objectives, responsibilities, economic principles, business integrity, political activity, health, safety and the environment, community, competition and communication.

Source: *Shell* (www)

Pfizer: To achieve our Purpose and Mission we affirm our values of Integrity, Leadership, Innovation, Performance, Teamwork, Customer Focus, Respect for People and Community.

Source: *Pfizer* (www)

Tesco: Our two values drive the whole way we do business. No one tries harder for customers:

◆ Understand customers better than anyone

◆ Be energetic, be innovative and be first for customers

◆ Use our strengths to deliver unbeatable values to our customers

◆ Look after our people so they can look after our customers – 'Treat people how we like to be treated'

◆ There's one team... The Tesco Team

◆ Trust and respect each other

◆ Strive to do our very best

◆ Give support to each other and praise more than criticise

◆ Ask more than tell and share knowledge so that it can be used

◆ Enjoy work, celebrate success and learn from experience.

Source: *Tesco* (www)

Analysing the environment

Analysing the environment involves examining the current capabilities of the organisation and the trends in the external environment that will impact on the organisation. Analysis is a key feature of developing a strategy. Strategy without analysis is like going trekking without a map; analysis without strategy is just thought without action.

Analysis of the current situation may show that the organisation needs to revisit its mission and goals, or it may lead directly to the development of strategic goals and plans.

Here is what the process of environmental analysis and making strategic plans became at General Electric, a company renowned for strategic planning.

Strategic planning at General Electric in the Jack Welch era
Jack Welch's tenure (1981–1998) at the head of General Electric is considered one of the finest examples of corporate leadership in history. His mission when he took over was to create a company that was the most profitable, highly diversified company on earth with world-quality leadership in all of its product lines. His core value was quality. His goals were reinvestment in productivity and quality in core businesses, staying on the leading edge for high technology businesses, and growing in the service businesses by adding outstanding people to create new ventures and by making acquisitions.

His strategic analysis and planning were somewhat offbeat. Each business had to produce a 'playbook' every year with one-page answers to five business environment questions, such as 'What are your market dynamics globally today, and where are they going over the next several years?' These playbooks would then be discussed and agreed at a yearly half-day review. This simple analytical approach facilitated corporate understanding and corporate speed of movement. Business targets and financial planning were based on objectives, but were reasonably flexible as Welch believed set budgets could inhibit rather than stretch managers.

Source: *Adapted from Grant and Neupert* (1999)

Strategic goals and plans

Strategic goals show how to get to where you want to be, and plans specify where the organisation is going in a more definite or precise way. All good plans, of course, start with goals or objectives.

Oregon State University's mission is as follows:
Oregon State University aspires to stimulate a lasting attitude of inquiry, openness and social responsibility. To meet these aspirations, we are committed to providing excellent academic programs, educational experiences and creative scholarship.

Three strategic goals guide Oregon State University in meeting its mission

Statewide Campus
Oregon State University has a historic and unique role in Oregon. As a land-grant university, our heritage is articulated in the statement 'the State of Oregon is the campus of Oregon State University.' We emphasise the importance of extending the University into every community in Oregon. OSU will provide learning opportunities for Oregonians, and will create and apply knowledge that contributes to the prosperity of the State and its quality of life.

Compelling Learning Experience
Oregon State University is committed to creating an atmosphere of intellectual curiosity, academic freedom, diversity, and personal empowerment. This will enable everyone to learn with and from others. This compelling learning experience celebrates knowledge; encourages personal growth and awareness; acknowledges the benefits of diverse experiences, world views, learning styles, and values; and engenders personal and societal values that benefit the individual and society. OSU will develop curricula based on sound disciplinary knowledge and input from

practitioners. Students will acquire skills and knowledge for a lifetime of learning, and will be involved in scholarly and creative pursuits.

Top-Tier University
Oregon State University aspires to be a top-tier university. It is a Carnegie Research I University, a sea-grant institution and space-grant program, in addition to being a land-grant institution. We will measure our success by: the caliber of entering students, the accomplishments of students and alumni, the quality of the faculty, the quality of instructional and research facilities, the effectiveness and productivity of engagement with businesses and constituents, and the support for research and scholarship.

Source: *Oregon State University* (www)

Note the mention of measurement in Oregon State University's goals. Good goals or objectives should be measurable.

Cascading the strategy

In order to implement the strategy, it has to be translated into goals and plans at every level of the organisation. We can see this as a hierarchy of goals in Figure 1.4.

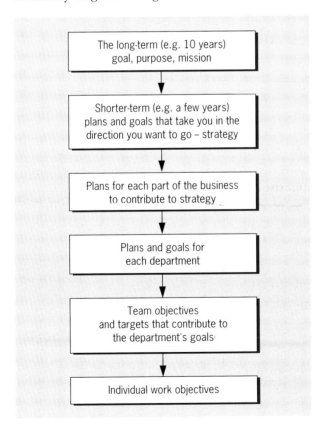

Figure 1.4 *A hierarchy of goals*

In this way every member of the organisation working at any level should be working to achieve objectives that contribute to the organisation reaching its overall goals. In other words, you have responsibility for implementing strategy as it is translated and made applicable to your area of control and influence. If you are not doing your bit, this could affect the organisation's overall performance. Business awareness in this case is knowing what your organisation's strategy is and what this means for your area of control and influence.

Business awareness is knowing what your organisation's strategy is and what it means you have to do. For example, if the corporate strategy is based on greater responsiveness to customer needs, have you done a customer profile of your department? If it is a commitment to quality, do you regularly update your health and safety risk assessments?

Activity 2
Strategy

Objectives

In this activity you will focus on your organisation's mission, values and strategic objectives. Use this activity to:

◆ identify your organisation's current vision, mission and values

◆ identify strategic objectives for your business, your work area and yourself.

While a mission is about the purpose and overall goals, a set of values can give the organisation the guiding principles that govern the way it will act.

Remember that:

◆ a vision is essentially a loose statement of intent or aim

◆ a mission is what has to be put in place to achieve the vision

◆ values are essentially idealistic policy guidelines for the organisation

◆ goals and objectives attempt to define where the organisation is going in a more definite or precise way.

Task

1 Examine your organisation's current vision/mission statement document. If you don't have one, then you can draw one up. Use organisational literature, sales information, annual report, etc. to find out what your organisation wants to achieve and how it proposes to get there.

To what extent does the mission statement define what the organisation is and what it is not? To what extent does it capture the distinguishing features of your organisation? Consider changing it to make it more accurate and up to date.

Current mission statement:

Does it capture your organisation?

2 Your organisation may produce a statement of its core values. Find out what these are. If there is no statement, think about what they should be to reflect the organisation's current culture and the messages senior management send out to others, both inside and outside the organisation.

Core values:

3 From the mission statement, the organisation can develop its strategic goals. These then cascade throughout the organisation and should be translated at each level if they are to be achieved.

Identify strategic goals and objectives for each of the headings below which cascade downwards from the mission.

For your organisation (these may be stated as part of your organisation's strategy):

For your department/work area:

For yourself:

Feedback

Here is an example:

The **vision** of the organisation is 'to be a world leader in PC and Internet software'.

The **mission statement** is 'to provide customers with the widest choice of quality PC and Internet software on the market at reasonable prices, delivered on time and supported by excellent customer service'.

The **values** come under the following headings: growth, innovation, customer service, quality, teamwork, productivity, security.

Key **strategic goals and objectives** are as follows:

For the organisation:

◆ to develop agreements, contracts and alliances with all the main software players to maximise product choice

◆ to develop a quality systems approach in the supply, processing and distribution of retail software.

For the department/work area (marketing):

◆ to develop a marketing plan to include online and offline marketing

◆ to work with IT to develop an attractive and focused e-commerce website.

For the manager:

◆ to devise a market e-survey to collect customer comments

◆ to develop a catalogue for online and offline purchasing.

A time-related element could be included in these objectives.

Note that these objectives are all related. The manager, by achieving his or her objectives, contributes to the organisation's strategic goals.

Check your responses with your colleagues. How far do you all agree on your answers?

To deepen your understanding of organisations' use of vision, mission statement and values, you could visit the websites of other organisations, such as:

Johnson & Johnson:
www.johnsonandjohnson.com – look particularly at this company's 'credo'

Nike:
www.nikebiz.com – look at responsibility

Honda:
www.world.honda.com/profile

What do your organisation's competitors say?

Why do you think some organisations may not state their missions?

◆ Recap

In this theme you have reviewed the nature of organisations and the process for strategic decision making.

Review the core components of your organisation and what makes it different from others

◆ Analysis of the nature and components of your organisation will help you to make decisions and take action.

- Internal and external environmental influences have implications for the organisation's direction and strategy.

Identify ways to communicate the goals of an organisation

- Every member of the organisation, working at any level, should be working to achieve objectives that contribute to the organisation reaching its overall goals.

- Capturing the distinguishing features of the organisation those that set it apart from its competitors, is key to producing a memorable goals.

Identify your organisation's vision, mission and values and how these translate into strategic objectives

- A starting point for strategy is to have a vision for the future.

- In order to implement the strategy, it has to be translated into goals and plans at every level of the organisation.

Develop a strategic understanding of your business

- Business awareness is knowing what your organisation's strategy is and what it means you have to do.

 **More @**

Campbell, D., Stonehouse, G. and Houston, B. (2002) 2nd edition, *Business Strategy: an Introduction*, Elsevier Butterworth-Heinemann
This is an accessible textbook that provides a straightforward and comprehensive guide to complex issues and concepts. Of particular relevance to this theme is Part 1 'An introduction to the strategic process'.

Dixon, R. (2003) 3rd edition, *The Management Task*, Elsevier Butterworth-Heinemann
This book considers the nature of management and the environment in which management operates. The requirements for effective, successful management techniques are explored, covering many areas from the need for planning and forecasting, leadership, motivation and communication to control and decision-making. See Part 2 'The Management Process' and Part 4 'The Managerial Environment' in particular.

Handy, C. (1993) 4th edition, *Understanding Organizations*, Penguin Books
This is a classic text that looks at organisational structures and cultures. It offers an illuminating discussion of key concepts of

1 The organisation in context

concern to all managers: culture, motivation, leadership, power, role-playing and working in groups.

Johnson, G. and Scholes, K. (1999) 5th edition, *Exploring Corporate Strategy*, Prentice Hall Europe
This is a classic work on corporate strategy. You may find it useful for future reference. Throughout the text, strategy is seen through three complementary 'lenses': 'design' (an analytical approach); 'experience' (builds on cultural, institutional and cognitive schools of thought); 'ideas' (builds on evolutionary and complexity theories).

Pascale, R., and Millemann, M. and Gioja, L. (2000) *Surfing the Edge of Chaos*, Texere Publishing Ltd or go to www.surfingchaos.com
Surfing the Edge of Chaos is an unusually good book on applying the lessons of complexity science to business progress. The material is aimed at continuous renewal of the large existing organisation, but will be valuable to organisations of all ages and sizes.

Full references are provided at the end of the book.

2 The organisational landscape

There are some key features in your organisational landscape that will help you to analyse your business environment.

Culture and structure are the building blocks that help us to identify the norms, beliefs, opinions, values and customs that are prevalent in an organisation. 'It's the way we do things around here.' An organisation's culture is reflected in or by the different structures of the organisation, which are the designated 'positions', roles and accountabilities of individuals.

The next perspective is on how different aspects of the internal environment affect the organisation and its ability to achieve its goals. This theme looks at:

◆ products and services

◆ people and their skills

◆ finance

◆ resources.

Your analysis of the landscape starts with the 'balanced scorecard' approach. This is a technique that is used to widen your perspective of an organisation to help determine the aspects that will deliver results in the future. The second technique explored assesses the products and services offered by your organisation. It is a strategic tool called portfolio analysis.

Within this theme you will:

◆ **Examine the culture and structural types within an organisation and how they operate as a vehicle for change**

◆ **Identify the key factors in an organisation that impact on its success**

◆ **Measure the performance of your organisation using the balanced scorecard approach**

◆ **Consider how portfolio analysis can help you analyse the products and services your organisation offers.**

The internal environment: culture and structure

A useful description of the different cultures found in organisations has been provided by Charles Handy in *Understanding Organizations* (1993). He distinguishes four types.

Cultural types

- **Power culture.** This depends upon a strong leader, with central power, manipulating all the activities of the organisation. Jack Welch, the former CEO of General Electric, and Rupert Murdoch, of News Corporation, spring to mind. Employees need to be able to relate well to the central power holder and to anticipate what is expected of them and perform accordingly. They must feel able to take risks. Their performance, loyalty and commitment to organisational goals will be well rewarded.

- **Role culture.** This is where roles are more important than individuals. In this kind of culture, logic and reason, impersonal systems and procedures rule behaviour. Large banks, government offices and insurance companies are examples of role cultures.

- **Task culture.** Here there is no single source of power and the work is the priority. The task culture depends upon getting the best and most creative individuals to work together towards organisational goals. Teamwork becomes paramount in achieving the organisation's mission. Technology companies and management consultancies are typical examples of the task culture.

- **Person culture.** The main concern of a person-centred culture is to look after the needs of the individuals. Often small groups of professionals may come together and design an organisation based around a person culture. The reason they do this is to enhance and develop their own personal aims and objectives and to share common facilities. Examples include barristers' chambers, architects' partnerships and small consultancies.

Structural types

The structure follows from the culture. So, based on the four Handy models, the following types of structure arise:

♦ **Power structure.** Handy likens this to a web. The boss is the key to advancement, not 'titles' or a hierarchy. Do well and you advance – fast. Mess up, and you could be out altogether. Jack Welch commented:

> We are now down in some businesses to four layers from the top to the bottom. That's the ultimate objective. We used to have things like department managers, section managers, subsection managers, unit managers, supervisors. We are driving these titles out... We used to go from CEO to sectors to groups to businesses. We now go from CEO...to businesses. Nothing else. There is nothing else there. Zero.
>
> When you take out layers, you change the exposure of the managers who remain. They sit right in the sun. Some of them blotch immediately – they can't stand the exposure. I firmly believe that an overburdened, overstretched executive is the best executive, because he or she doesn't have time to meddle, to deal in trivia, or to bother people.

Source: *Tichy and Charan* (1989)

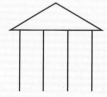

♦ **Role structure.** The role structure is sometimes called a bureaucratic one, though this is perhaps only where the role culture is taken to extremes, as in government departments. In a role structure, everyone has their designated job description, procedural handbook, accountabilities sheet, hierarchical career path, reward structure and so on. Handy sees this as a sturdy Greek temple.

♦ **Task structure.** This structure is associated with a flexible, project-based/matrix structure. Handy likens it to a net.

Project groups or teams are formed as the need arises, and are disbanded once their task is finished. It is very adaptable, egalitarian and quick to respond. Microsoft uses a task structure.

◆ **Person structure.** This is also egalitarian, though you would not say it is team based. Individuals are independent, and do not feel any particular loyalty. Examples include consultants in the NHS, computer programmers and IT people who work on short-term contracts. They only come together as a matter of convenience or self-interest. Handy sees this as a cluster or galaxy of mixed stars.

Horses for courses

Do not assume that any single culture or associated structure is better than any other, or that the models do not have wide varieties. For example, an organisation which outsources a lot of its activities could be a mixture of a task and person culture. Cultures and structures do change and there may be more than one variation within any single organisation.

The culture and structure of any organisation is influenced by various factors, such as:

◆ History and ownership – centralised ownership tends towards a power culture, as do family-owned companies. New organisations tend towards power or task-based cultures/structures.

◆ Size – larger organisations tend to be role based because they need to be kept under control, but they can also be power based. A smaller company may be power based, but could be person or task based.

◆ Technology – for example, rapidly changing technologies tend to be associated with task-based organisations. Routine, programmable operations are more suited to being role based.

◆ Goals and objectives – this relates to strategic direction. A key point is that strategic goals and objectives can change cultures and structures. How many times do you hear about organisations going through a culture change?

♦ People – cautious people may work better in a role culture. Risk takers may prefer a power culture. Highly skilled people may prefer the person culture.

♦ External environment – different nationalities, for example, have different cultural tendencies which affect the way they behave organisationally. Japan, with its paternalistic culture, has a tendency to the task-based organisation, whereas the UK's individualistic streak produces more power or person structures, as evidenced by the number of its small and medium-sized enterprises (SMEs). Political systems also affect culture and structure.

Organisation 2005 – Procter & Gamble unveils massive culture-change exercise

Mumbai, India, Oct 11: There's something different about Procter & Gamble: It's culture. The hushed voices give way to loud guffaws more often, ties are optional, and – forgive the nit-picking – but now, everyone is allowed to use bone-china cups for tea. Make no mistake though: The new-look P&G, which is slowly emerging from behind the shadows, has made more than just cosmetic changes.

Instead, for the last one year, the elephant has been painstakingly learning how to dance nimbly to the tune of a new global corporate motto: 'An organisation driven by Stretch, Innovation and Speed (SIS), towards breakthrough goals.'

The P&G mambo began in September 1998, when The Procter & Gamble Company (US) announced major global structural changes under the 'Organisation 2005: The mission to take P&G's global turnover from $38 billion to a targeted $70 billion, by 2005'. It's taken a year of churning and burning, but the dust clouds of uncertainty are finally settling – and slowly the new culture based on Speed, Innovation and Stretch is seeping in.

Accompanying the new look corporate culture is a new look corporate office: Here, the walls will be plastered with the brighter, fresher P&G ethos and the windows will be firmly left open to let the winds of change rush in. In an initiative called 'Project Pride', P&G-ites are designing the office for themselves. Come July 2000, the 350-odd P&G employees in Mumbai will move in under one self-designed roof.

Catching up with P&G on its road to change – in an exclusive, detailed, two-part account – The Financial Express traces the lives and times of two livewire teams – P&G's Culture Team and Pride Team – who have been silently and swiftly driving the change management initiatives in P&G India for the last one year.

Their mandate was large – to get the lumbering P&G to limber up – their means, small incremental steps: from Clean-up Days, to reward schemes, to new ground rules, to team-based performance evaluation. But one year down the line, the change is evident. On the back of motivated employees, P&G India is Speeding towards its Stretch goal, with Innovative initiatives. The elephant is not just facing the music – but also dancing to the new beat of Mambo No. 2005.

Source: *Singh* (1999)

Why are culture and structure relevant to managers?

There are certain types of organisational cultures and structures, and internal and external environmental factors influence which ones are adopted or develop. How do you fit into your organisational culture as a manager? For example, if you are in a power culture/structure, are you taking enough risks to try to improve your position? Why not break the budget rather than religiously following it? If you are in a task culture, are you happy with teamworking? Is a role culture too restricting for you? Is a person culture too independent?

If your organisation's culture and structure are changing due to internal and external pressures, how do these changes affect you and your decisions? Do you know what is expected of you? How do you find out?

What influence do you have on the culture and organisational structure? Perhaps more than you think. If you are moving towards a task-based culture, have you tried new teamworking techniques? Should you have a dress-down day? Is there a case for outsourcing in your department?

The activities that follow provide a framework for assessing your organisation's culture, and a case study to explore structure as a vehicle for change.

Activity 3
Assess your organisation's culture and structure

Objective

Use this activity to assess your organisation's culture.

Charles Handy (1993) developed a working model of culture based on:

◆ **power** – where the strong leader, with central power, manipulates all the activities of the organisation

◆ **role** – where roles are more important than individuals, for example in bureaucratic organisations

◆ **task** – here there is no single source of power and the project is the key

◆ **person** – the main concern of a person-centred culture is to look after the needs of the individuals within it.

Source: *Handy* (1993)

Remember that this is a working model. Your own organisation might be a mixture of two or more types of culture.

Task

1   Explain your organisation's culture using Handy's model.

2   Do different cultural types exist or overlap in the organisation? If so, why do you think this is?

Your organisation's culture:

Different cultural types:

Feedback

Handy's model is a guide. Cultures and structures may be multi-layered and complex. Talk to your colleagues about your findings and discuss how far your organisational culture and structure empowers or restrains individuals to make decisions.

Activity 4
Structural change

Objective

This activity is based on a case study. Use the activity to explore structure as a vehicle for change.

Case study

Read the case study below.

Northwestern Memorial Hospital Announces Corporate Reorganization

The Northwestern Memorial Corporation board unanimously approved a move to streamline the corporate structure and change its name to Northwestern Memorial HealthCare. The matter was decided at the board's Jan. 17 meeting.

Under the new structure, multiple business subsidiaries and functions will be merged into Northwestern Memorial Hospital and will be governed by the newly titled Northwestern Memorial HealthCare and its board of directors. The reorganization also expands the role of Northwestern Memorial Foundation – the fundraising arm of Northwestern Memorial HealthCare.

'We want to create a model for innovate healthcare management,' said Gary Mecklenburg, president of Northwestern Memorial HealthCare and chief executive officer of Northwestern Memorial Hospital. 'The new structure allows for quicker decision-making and greater flexibility – elements we need to excel in today's complex, fast-paced healthcare environment.'

Additionally, an Office of the CEO has been created. Gary Mecklenburg is president and chief executive officer of Northwestern Memorial HealthCare and chief executive officer of Northwestern Memorial Hospital. Kathy Murray has become the chief operating officer and executive vice president of

Northwestern Memorial HealthCare. Dean Harrison has been named president of Northwestern Memorial Hospital.

'This organization more accurately describes how we have been managing the hospital and the corporation for some time,' Mr Mecklenburg said. 'Northwestern Memorial values teamwork, and Kathy and I are pleased to have Dean join us in setting the direction of this organization. It gives us greater management strength now and for the future.'...

'Northwestern Memorial's previous corporate structure was established in 1982 in response to meet federal regulations at that time,' Mr Mecklenburg said. 'It served us well for 18 years. This new structure will better align the organization with our mission and enable us to do what we do best: focus on patient care, research, education and community service,' Mr Mecklenburg said.

The board members for the former subsidiaries will continue to play important roles with the new Northwestern Memorial HealthCare, particularly in 'strengthening our leadership in research, education and community service,' Mr Mecklenburg said.

Source: *PRNewswire Association* (2001)

Task

1 Summarise the structural changes at Northwestern Memorial Hospital.

2 Explain why these changes were made.

Structural changes:

Why these changes were made:

Feedback

You may have noted some of these structural changes:

- The name has been changed to Northwestern Memorial HealthCare
- Subsidiaries and functions have been merged and are governed by Northwestern Memorial HealthCare and its board of directors
- Northwestern Memorial Foundation has expanded its role
- A new Office of the CEO has been created.

Here are some possible reasons for making these changes:

- To create a model for innovative healthcare management
- To allow for quicker decision making and greater flexibility
- To give greater management strength now and for the future
- To align the organisation with the mission and enable it to do what it does best: patient care, research, education and community service
- To strengthen its leadership in research, education and community service.

Internal capabilities

The development of strategy involves looking at the organisation's existing capabilities and constraints. Some organisations periodically carry out a systematic internal audit to take stock of their current situation. You may have a good view of the capabilities of your organisation from the point of view of your role as a manager of a particular part of the business. However, it is helpful to widen this perspective and look at the internal environment as a whole. You may find that there are resources or expertise in another part of the organisation that you could use. This section examines how different aspects of the internal environment affect the organisation and its ability to achieve its goals.

An alternative way of looking at the internal environment was developed to show the interaction between the key elements of an organisation. This is called the Seven S model. The Seven Ss are strategy, structure, staff, systems, style, skills, and shared values. If you want to find out more about it, you could search the Internet using the key words '7 s model' or 'seven s model'.

Source: *Peters and Waterman* (1982)

Products and services

An organisation can be defined by the products and services it provides. After all, that is why it is in business. These products and services are distinctive in some way to the organisation that supplies them – whether the distinction be brand, price, quality or location.

Clearly, any changes to an organisation's products and services will have an impact on its ability to compete.

> In 1991, Gerald Ratner famously described one of the products of his chain of jewellery shops – a sherry decanter – as 'total crap'. It caused a furore. The share price plummeted, customers and shareholders were outraged, and the tabloids could not hide their delight at his misfortune. The business went under within two years of the remark.
>
> Ratner, as CEO, altered the perception of his product in just two words. This example shows, in an extreme way, how factors within the organisation can affect its fortune.

Decisions about products and services are vital. If you do not update your product range and your overall offer to customers, there is a danger you may get left behind. For example, many out-of-town supermarkets now have 24-hour opening to cater for customers' changing lifestyles. However, if you do update your range, people may not like it. British Airways famously changed its aircrafts' distinctive, sober livery and brought in multicoloured, abstract designs for the aircrafts' tail fins. No one seemed to like this, and the decision was reversed.

Managers have to be aware of what makes their products sell and be constantly alert to changes in the perceptions and expectations of their customers. That is why product analysis is so useful.

See the section on Portfolio analysis.

People and their skills

An organisation's people are not just employees. They include directors and shareholders, customers who buy from you and suppliers who sell to you. Indeed they include all the people the organisation influences and is influenced by. All these people are 'stakeholders'.

However, you may care to define an organisation by the people who work in it – their knowledge, talent and skills. The wrong blend and the organisation is in trouble. A shortage of specialist skills and the organisation is in trouble. A lack of harmony between employers and employees and the organisation is in trouble.

Can employees really make a difference to the success of an organisation?

Research in the US and UK has suggested that there is some correlation between people management practices and the bottom line (profitability). Mark Huselid of Rutgers University, New Jersey, has developed and extensively tested an index of sophisticated people-management practices. He found in one company that a small increase in the index is associated with a 7.05 per cent decrease in staff turnover, a $27,000 increase in sales and a $3,800 increase in profits (Baron and Collard, 1999).

A particular tool that enables an organisation to focus on the importance of people (employees) is the balanced scorecard.

See the section on the balanced scorecard.

Finance

Organisations have many different ways to finance their ongoing development – loans, bonds, equity, selling assets, retained earnings, funding – and the choice may impact significantly on their development. For example, in 2000 the telecommunications industry spent billions via debt issue, bonds, to pay for the licences for the next generation of mobile phones. This is a significant risk, especially as there is some doubt as to the potential of, and demand for, a third generation (3G) network. In 2001, British Telecom (BT) had to sell some of its assets to cover its over-geared position.

The following case study demonstrates (in an extreme way) how the financial structuring of an organisation – 'leverage', in this case, which is borrowing to finance investment or speculation – can affect cash flow (liquidity) and even the very survival of the organisation.

Long Term Capital Management (LTCM), run by John Meriweather, was a hedge fund boasting two Nobel prizewinning economics professors. They developed a 'perfect' mathematical risk model for maximising returns based on high leverage and arbitrage (exploiting discrepancies in stock price spreads). From 1994 to 1998, LTCM made spectacular returns for its 100 or so investors. But then the model stopped working, and financing its positions by huge borrowings backfired. The markets in Brazil, Indonesia and Russia crashed, leaving LTCM out on a limb. With no liquidity and a $1 trillion credit gap, its collapse threatened to bring down the US and global banking system. A consortium of banks prompted by the US Federal Reserve had to step in to bail it out. By contrast with this, Nick Leeson's actions in bringing down Barings bank seem somewhat tame.

It is not every manager who gets the chance to have such a dramatic effect on their organisation or the external environment! Most likely, where you do have impact is in the budgets you have allocated to finance your part of the operations. The way you operate this budget is important. If you are over the budget, costs go up. Lack of control over costs can seriously affect what the organisation can do to improve its performance.

Resources

An organisation's resources – such as land, buildings, systems, processes – play a key part in determining its strategic approach. They represent what it can do and what it cannot do. An organisation using natural resources, for example, will need to have a steady stream of new sources so that as old sources dry up, new ones come on line. It also has to make sure that its resources and the way it uses them are as efficient as its competitors. Witness the demise of the UK coal industry or the decline of the horse and carriage. Hence, research and development (R&D) and information technology (IT) are important to enable the organisation to keep ahead.

Many organisations realise that they have processes to which they can add value in different ways. For example, retailers have customers on their databases who regularly buy their products. This allows them to diversify their product range and sell them new services and products, such as financial services. For example, the UK supermarket Tesco is now moving into selling car insurance. Other organisations may have resources to which they cannot add value, so they may sell them or outsource to people who can utilise those resources more efficiently.

Boots hopes to make strides in US with deal
BOOTS yesterday signalled its intention to take on the US market with the £233 million acquisition of Clearasil, the acne treatment, from Procter & Gamble. The healthcare and pharmacy group hopes that the purchase – which represents its largest product acquisition in a decade – will provide it with a US launch pad. The company said it hoped initially to sell a range of other skin products through the same retailers that market Clearasil. Eventually Boots hopes to use the network of supermarkets, chemists and mass-market drugstores to distribute other products such as Strepsils throat lozenges. However, in line with the recent decision to close down Boots stand-alone outlets in The Netherlands, there are no plans to establish Boots stores in America. Barry Clare, managing director of BHI, the Boots division that develops over-the-counter drugs, said: 'The Clearasil acquisition is an excellent strategic fit, substantially increasing our global scale and coverage. It enables us to leverage

our skincare technology and also broaden distribution to drugstore and grocery channels.'

Source: The Times (2000)

In this case study notice how Boots aims to use its resources to best advantage. The company has acquired a product which enables it not just to increase its product base, but also to utilise its skincare technology more efficiently and take advantage of broader distribution channels – all this without increasing its own retail outlets.

Activity 5
The internal environment

Objective

This activity will help you to identify the impact of internal factors on organisational success.

Case study

This case study considers all the factors in the internal environment that affect an organisation's strategy:

◆ culture and structure

◆ products and services

◆ people and their skills

◆ finance

◆ resources.

Read through the case study before you complete the task.

First Union's Design For Bank Insurance Success

If the key to First Union's success in insurance sales could be summed up in a single word, that word would be change. Change customer thinking. Change the sales culture. Change delivery. Change the pace of activity.

First Union has become an agent of change as it has moved more aggressively to integrate insurance into its financial services. The learning curve over the past four years has been steep – and so has the success curve.

For background, the First Union Insurance Group has more than one million customers and 4,000 licensed agents. For four years, we have led the nation in annuity sales and are on track to match or exceed last year's record sales of $2.2 billion. We are strong in credit insurance, term life sales are showing excellent yearly gains, and individual and group life-health and personal and commercial property-casualty are on a healthy track.

First Union was the first bank to deliver insurance via the Internet and, with the recent addition of Pivot.com, is now well positioned to capitalize on the explosion in e-commerce.

Change does not come easily. Banks and insurance companies are far more comfortable with what has worked in the past than what might work in the future.

To keep up with the changing landscape, First Union has developed these key strategies:

Shift customer attitudes and assumptions. Although the financial services industry is attuned to legislative and regulatory changes that allow banks, brokerages and insurance companies to compete, customers are not necessarily aware of them. Therefore, communication is a high priority.

When consumers know that a bank is one option where they can handle their insurance needs, they respond. National studies by Synergistics Research Corp. and the American Council of Life Insurance show that two of three auto/home insurance buyers are likely to purchase through a bank while 45 percent are likely to purchase life insurance through one.

To communicate First Union's insurance capabilities to such customers, we insert marketing stuffers in statements and make materials available in bank branches and brokerage offices. Telemarketing, trade shows, seminars to reach non-customers, and internal communication tools to our 72,000 employees round out the effort.

Most importantly, we are giving the non-insurance sales forces – the branch-based financial advisors, our 7,000-strong brokerage team – excellent materials to use and share.

Educate the sales force. We educate them on the nature of insurance products, how to match products to customer needs and how to deliver them efficiently. We have worked with the sales force on how to engage customers in a positive manner about the need for protection against adversity through the purchase of insurance.

Blend full service and self-service. There always will be people, particularly the more affluent, who want a friendly face across the table. But we are seeing a growing preference, especially among younger people, for more impersonal, cyberspace relationships that they can control. These customers value independence, convenience and low cost.

We've built platforms for both of those preferences, as well as one that fits in the middle.

We are reaching out to more affluent customers by offering personal service. The selling point here is the opportunity to work with an institution the customer trusts and to blend insurance into an overall financial plan that is securely under one roof. Our team focuses on insurance products valued from $250,000 to $1 million.

The middle-ground platform is First Union Direct, a call center that offers customers someone who can talk them through options, but with no one knocking on the door. Callers target mass- and middle-market customers with products that include term, whole, universal and variable life insurance; long-term care; and some forms of disability insurance.

First Union's online Insurance Center lets customers and non-customers research, select and purchase a range of products. The site offers quoting from multiple carriers as well as do-it-yourself planning tools, educational information from experts, a glossary of insurance terms and links to ratings and buyers' guides.

This site is the result of our acquisition of Pivot.com, a young company that specialized in moving the entire insurance process – research, selection, fulfillment and customer service – onto the Web. Pivot lets First Union provide consumers with electronic access to insurance and allows us to partner with other financial services companies that want to offer insurance under their own label.

Simplify the process. When an applicant fills out one electronic form at First Union, we can use that data over and over. The next time the customer wants a product, the form that appears can have most of the information already filled in.

Furthermore, we now have the capability to send data electronically rather than shooting paper back and forth. This not only cuts down on customer application annoyance, but it also is a bottom-line benefit for us.

Looking ahead, we see tremendous opportunities on the commercial and individual sides of insurance. The heavyweight on the opportunity scale is the existing base of First Union customers –15 million individuals, institutions and corporations who already use First Union for at least one financial service. It is far easier to talk to a friend than a stranger, and we have friends all over the nation.

Source: *De Gorter* (2000)

Task

Using the table provided, identify the strategy of First Union. Then, under each category, list the different ways First Union is using its internal environment to achieve success.

Key elements of the strategy:

Internal environment	*Ways to utilise factors to achieve success*
Culture and structure	
Products and services	
People and their skills	
Finance	
Resources	

Feedback

Your table might look something like this.

Key elements of the strategy:
Develop a change strategy
Shift customer attitudes and assumptions
Educate the sales force
Blend full service and self-service
Simplify the process

Internal environment	Ways to utilise factors to achieve success
Culture and structure	Sales culture
	Change culture
	Learning culture
	Task/role structure
Products and services	Strong in annuity sales, credit insurance, term life sales, individual and group life-health and personal and commercial property-casualty
	First to deliver insurance via the Internet
	Multi-platform services
People and their skills	1 million customers
	72,000 employees, 4,000 licensed agents, 7,000 brokers
	Well-trained employees
Finance	Sales of $2.2 billion
Resources	Pivot.com
	First Union Direct call center
	Online Insurance Center
	Electronic systems and processes

To build on your work in this activity you can look at the internal factors in your organisation and how they influence its performance and strategic direction.

The balanced scorecard

This section explains a technique that is used to analyse the internal environment, to evaluate its impacts and make decisions.

What is the balanced scorecard?

Traditionally, organisations used financial measures to assess the organisation's success. It is clearly essential for the organisation to meet the needs of owners and creditors and to ensure that it has adequate cash flow and liquidity, but using financial measures alone may leave it in a weak position for the future. If the efforts of the organisation are focused on achieving financial objectives, what happens to the initiatives that help it to perform well in the future, such as training and development, keeping customers satisfied and improving internal processes? It is useful to note that financial results only indicate past performance – you have to look at other aspects of an organisation to get a feel for what will happen in the future.

The balanced scorecard can be used to widen the perspective of an organisation so that it focuses on the organisational aspects that will deliver results in the future, as well as on the financial requirements. It was invented in the early 1990s by Dr Robert Kaplan of Harvard Business School and Dr David Norton of Renaissance Solutions Inc. It is a strategic management tool which focuses on four aspects of the business to create a 'balanced' perspective:

◆ Financial – budgets and financial results, for example

◆ Internal business processes – are the organisation's operations producing products and services which conform to quality standards and customer requirements?

◆ Customer – is the business customer focused?

◆ Learning and growth – the organisation's attitudes to employee training and development and learning.

The balanced scorecard can be used to interpret the organisation's vision and strategy for each of these perspectives and to set up objectives and measures to assess performance (hence 'scorecard'). By setting measurable objectives for each perspective, an organisation is recognising and working on the areas of the organisation that it knows will deliver results in the future. For example, if you actively seek to improve customer service, you will reap the benefits in terms of more satisfied customers who will repeat their business with you or recommend you to their friends.

The balanced scorecard is usually represented by a diagram (see Figure 2.1).

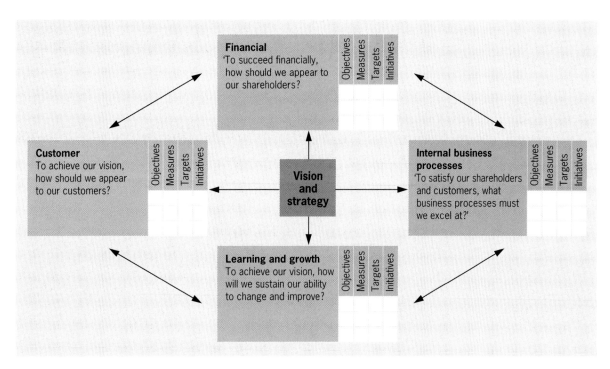

Figure 2.1 *The balanced scorecard*   Source: *Kaplan and Norton* (1996)

How it works

There are four key elements to the scorecard, as you can see from the diagram:

◆ Objectives or goals – what your strategy is

◆ Measures – the measure you are using, otherwise how will you know you have achieved your objectives?

◆ Targets – quantify your measure in terms of expected results

◆ Initiatives – strategic plans to achieve objectives and targets.

To develop a balanced scorecard, you need to do the following:

◆ Use the organisation's mission and strategy to identify the key objectives your business needs to achieve in each of the four perspectives

◆ Quantify these objectives so that you can measure the achievement of the objectives

◆ Plan how to make sure these objectives can be achieved

◆ Plan how to monitor and review the achievement of these objectives using the measures

◆ Review the results, publicise progress and take action to make improvements

◆ Regularly evaluate the objectives you have set so that they continue to be relevant to you.

The balanced scorecard can get quite complicated from a quantitative viewpoint. There are balanced scorecard software programs available to specifically deal with all the measurements and to analyse them. However, if you can keep it simple, it does give you a good way of analysing your internal environment and making decisions based on the outcomes.

Activity 6
The balanced scorecard

Objective

This is one of two activities that focus on internal environmental analysis, the other is portfolio analysis. Use this activity to assess the value of the balanced scorecard approach and analyse how it works. Later you will look at portfolio analysis.

Task

You may want to use external resources such as www.balancedscorecard.org or Kaplan and Norton (1992) to complete this task.

1   List five benefits of the balanced scorecard approach for organisations.

2   Draw up some objectives for your department using the balanced scorecard approach.

    First think about what your department needs to achieve in order to contribute to your organisation's strategy, both now and in the future. Then identify some objectives for each perspective.

Five benefits of the balanced scorecard approach:

◆

◆

◆

◆

◆

Objectives for your department:

Feedback

1 Your list of benefits of the balanced scorecard approach could include the following:

- ◆ It facilitates a balanced approach to strategy by focusing on more than just financial results

- ◆ It harmonises objectives, measures and targets, and strategic initiatives

- ◆ It ensures outcomes can be measured

- ◆ It improves the bottom line by focusing on targets that affect future performance

- ◆ It enables benchmarking of outcomes with other organisations.

2 You may find it helpful to discuss your objectives with colleagues. What are the implications for implementing these objectives? What benefits would you hope to achieve? How practical is it for your department to achieve these objectives?

Portfolio analysis

Portfolio analysis is a strategic tool used to assess the products and services offered by your organisation. It suggests you should think of your products and services as a portfolio(s) of options. How well is each of them doing? Should you sell or should you hold? Perhaps even buy...?

Fortune Brands Exploring Strategic Options for its Office Products Business – *Plan to Narrow Business Focus is Part of Ongoing Portfolio Analysis; Goals Include Sharp Increase in Shareholder Returns*

41

Fortune Brands, Inc. (www.fortunebrands.com), a leading consumer brands company, today announced that it is exploring strategic options for its ACCO World Corporation office products unit.

The evaluation, which includes the possible sale of the office products business, is a result of the company's ongoing strategic review of its portfolio of brands and businesses initiated earlier this year. 'This plan to narrow the focus of our consumer products portfolio is a bold step in the evolution of Fortune Brands and reflects our unrelenting commitment to sharply increasing returns and enhancing shareholder value,' said Chairman and Chief Executive Officer Norm Wesley. 'In 1999, we delivered on that commitment with a series of aggressive actions to reduce our cost structure and optimize operating efficiencies. Earlier this year, we began an intensive strategic review of our portfolio to ensure that Fortune Brands delivers even stronger results for our shareholders in the years ahead.

'Our aim in pursuing strategic options for our office products unit is to promote two key long-term objectives: generating a significant leap in our returns and strengthening our growth profile by focusing on our most attractive markets. And in the event of an office products divestiture, we expect that our near-term priority for the proceeds would be to immediately enhance shareholder value with high-return share repurchases and debt repayment, subject to market conditions,' Wesley added.

'ACCO is an industry leader that has made many important contributions to Fortune Brands' success over the years. However, ACCO competes in an industry that will likely benefit from consolidation and we don't see ourselves making that kind of commitment to office products. With its excellent brands and great people, we're optimistic that in the event of a divestiture, ACCO will be a valuable building block for success in that environment.'

Source: *Business Wire* (2000)

Dogs and other animals

The most famous portfolio analysis was devised by the Boston Consulting Group (BCG). It is called the BCG matrix (see Figure 2.2) and views an organisation's products as either:

- **dogs** – low market share, little potential growth
- **problem children** (or question marks)– low market share, high potential growth
- **cash cows** – high market share, low potential growth
- **stars** – high market share, high potential growth.

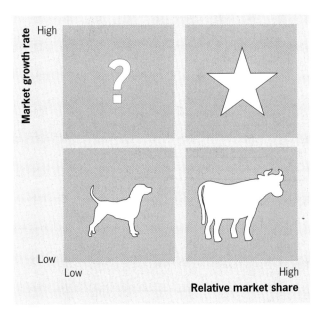

Figure 2.3 *The BCG matrix*   Source: *Baston Consulting Group* (1977)

The idea is that you assess each of your products in relation to this grid. Then, depending on what you find, you drop the dogs, milk the cash cows, develop the problem children and sustain the stars.

Like all portfolios, there should be a balance of each element. Dogs are on their way out, whilst problem children and stars have to be nurtured to ensure they deliver or continue to deliver. The cash cows are bringing in the money now and will help to build the stars and problem children. Too many problem children and stars can be a financial and management strain. Not enough means you may not be building enough future cash cows and will have insufficient cows to finance future development.

Although the BCG matrix is used to assess the organisation's product portfolio, it can also be used by large corporations or conglomerates to assess the portfolio of companies or business units within the group.

Managers and dogs

It is easy to see large groups like retailers having a field day using portfolio analysis on their products, or someone like Richard Branson with his Virgin empire. At this level, something is always coming in or going out as the portfolio is periodically assessed.

What about the average manager, though? How can portfolio analysis help you?

No matter which level you are at, you are responsible in some way for the product or service you provide for customers. You have an impact.

You could think of the products and services you provide to your internal customers as a portfolio. Which ones are growing in importance, which shrinking? Which ones can be improved? Which should be dropped? This type of thought process can keep you alert to change and keep you action focused.

Activity 7
Portfolio analysis

Objective

This is the second of two activities that focus on internal environmental analysis. Use it to analyse your organisation using the BCG matrix.

Task

1 Use the chart below to check your understanding of the BCG matrix – match the categories in the BCG matrix to the explanations by drawing connecting lines or arrows. Check your answers before going on to the next part of the task.

BCG matrix categories	Explanations
Dogs	High market share, low potential growth
Problem children	High market share, high potential growth
Cash cows	Low market share, high potential growth
Stars	Low market share, little potential growth

2 Assess five or six of your organisation's products/services using the BCG matrix provided.

Place them in the appropriate cells of the grid based on their potential growth and level of market share as defined above. Talk to your marketing department or senior management if you are unsure of the strength/weakness of any of the brands you have.

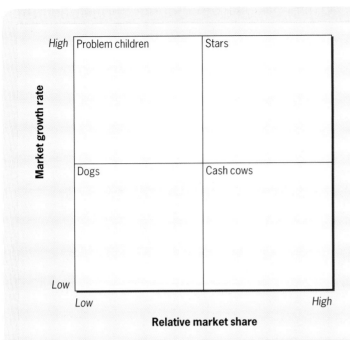

Source: *Boston Consulting Group* (1977)

3 Make some suggestions for what to do next with these
products/services.

Suggestions:

Feedback

1 Your chart should look like this.

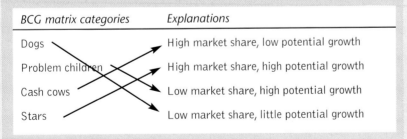

2 Discuss your assessment with your colleagues (perhaps in
your marketing department) to see if they agree with you.

3 As regards what to do next, the general idea is that you drop
the dogs, milk the cash cows, develop the problem children
and sustain the stars. Discuss your more detailed suggestions
with colleagues.

◆ Recap

In this theme you have looked at the landscape that impacts on the way your organisation operates.

Examine the culture and structural types within an organisation and how they operate as a vehicle for change

◆ Cultural and structural types have been defined by Charles Handy as being based on a power culture, a role culture, a task culture or a person culture. You may find that your organisation exhibits more than one type of culture.

◆ Culture and structure are influenced by history and ownership, size, technology, goals and objectives, people and the external environment. A knowledge of the culture, structure and context of the organisation can support decision making and make the adoption of change easier to manage.

Identify the key factors in an organisation that impact on its success

◆ The key factors that impact on the success of an organisation are the products and services, people and their skills, finance and resources.

◆ Decisions about strategy and new directions need to take each of these factors into account. Decisions about improvements to the way you work also need to include an analysis of each of the factors to see where changes could benefit the organisation.

Measure the performance of your organisation using the balanced scorecard approach

◆ The balanced scorecard can be used to widen the perspective of an organisation so that it focuses on the aspects of the organisation that will deliver results in the future.

◆ The balanced scorecard can be used to interpret the organisation's vision and strategy for each of the perspectives it takes. By setting measurable objectives for each perspective is the organisation is working on the areas of the business that will make a difference.

Consider how portfolio analysis can help you analyse the products and services your organisation offers

◆ Portfolio analysis examines the value and performance of your products and services.

◆ The BCG matrix views an organisation's products or services as either dogs, problem children, cash cows or stars.

◆ The general idea is that you drop the dogs, milk the cash cows, develop the problem children and sustain the stars.

▶▶ More @

Campbell, D., Stonehouse, G. and Houston, B. (2002) 2nd edition, *Business Strategy: an Introduction*, Elsevier Butterworth-Heinemann
This is an accessible textbook that provides a straightforward and comprehensive guide to complex issues and concepts. Take a look at Part 2 Chapter 3 'Human resources and culture'.

Handy, C. (1993) 4th edition, *Understanding Organizations, Penguin Books*, 180–216
This is a classic text that looks at organisational structures and cultures. It offers an illuminating discussion of key concepts of concern to all managers: culture, motivation, leadership, power, role-playing and working in groups.

Dixon, R. (2003) 3rd edition, *The Management Task*, Elsevier Butterworth-Heinemann
This book considers the nature of management and the environment in which management operates. The requirements for effective, successful management techniques are explored, covering many areas from the need for planning and forecasting, leadership, motivation and communication to control and decision making.

Williamson, D., Jenkins, W., Cooke, P. and Moreton, K.M. (2004) *Strategic Management and Business Analysis*, Elsevier Butterworth-Heinemann
This text provides a road map for the strategic analysis of a company or organisation. It identifies the key strategic questions and provides clear guidance on how they may be answered. See Part 1, 'The Four Big Questions You Need to Ask', and Part 2 'Helping You answer the Four Big Questions' for an analysis of organisation structure, strategic processes and competitive advantage.

The Balanced Scorecard Institute at www.balancedscorecard.org
To find out more about the balanced scorecard, check out The Balanced Scorecard Institute's website. This is a US non-profit-making organisation which focuses on applications of the balanced scorecard approach in government and other non-profit organisations. Or read **R. S. Kaplan and D. P. Norton (1996), *The Balanced Scorecard: Translating Strategy into Action*, Harvard Business School Press**.

Full references are provided at the end of the book.

3   The key players

Organisations cannot exist without people – people inside and outside the organisation who are all linked by its activities. This theme widens the perspective to look at the players in the organisation, the marketplace and the industry sector. The first of these players are the stakeholders. This is a broad term that typically encompasses any individual (or group) who affect or are affected by the performance of an organisation. You will examine your roles and responsibilities in relation to stakeholders

The focus then turns to your place in the market. Here you assess your customers and potential customers so that you can effectively target them with your products and services. Using market research and tools such as the Ansoff matrix will help to ensure that you make the most of the markets available to you.

Industry analysis focuses on the competitive situation within an industry or sector. We explore two approaches to industry analysis – the Five Force model and benchmarking. You will review the competitive forces in your industry and look beyond your own organisation to see how other key players in the industry operate.

Within this theme you will:

◆ **Carry out a stakeholder analysis for your organisation**

◆ **Assess how the marketplace works in terms of price, supply and demand**

◆ **Identify the purpose and nature of market research used by your organisation and how it aids decision making**

◆ **Apply the Ansoff matrix to identify possible opportunities in the market**

◆ **Analyse the competitive nature of your industry and carry out a Five Force analysis**

◆ **Consider benchmarking as an industry analysis tool.**

Stakeholders

Stakeholder theory says that stakeholders are those people and groups who are affected by, and affect, the performance of the organisation.

Stakeholders can be grouped according to their broadly shared interests, such as:

◆ owners, shareholders, investors

◆ employees

- managers
- suppliers
- customers
- regulators
- creditors
- local community.

Government, unions, interest groups, trade bodies and society as a whole can also be seen as stakeholders.

Figure 3.1 *Stakeholders*

The organisation has varying degrees of responsibility to these groups. For example:

- owners/shareholders – to maximise shareholder value, that is, growth and dividend
- employees – to provide wages and benefits, work satisfaction, safe and healthy working environment, continuous learning, etc.
- customers – to deliver quality products and services
- suppliers – to honour contracts
- creditors – to pay on time
- community – to safeguard the environment and provide local work
- government – to pay taxes and obey company and employment law
- regulators – to follow industry rules and codes of practice.

One of the problems with stakeholders is that the requirements and expectations of different groups may conflict.

English football clubs cannot decide which of their stakeholders they should please first. Plcs want to provide shareholder value, but the club managers have to keep buying players to keep the fans happy. The players want more money and greater freedom of contract, which upsets the boards. So the clubs make alliances with merchandisers and TV companies to maximise income, and the players want a slice of that too. When the Premier League clubs sign a TV deal, the larger clubs have to put up with the smaller clubs maintaining they do not get enough of the collective pie. BSkyB wants to be supplier and owner, but the regulator says this is a conflict of interest, so it can only own 9.9 per cent of a club. Some clubs want to expand their grounds, but the long-suffering local community will not let them. It has had enough of parked cars, fish and chip paper, broken bottles, urine and gratuitous abuse. But the local vendors are not complaining.

Some fans insist on standing up during the game, as they cannot get excited sitting down, which brings a threat of action on health and safety grounds from the local council. Players want more money, so they leave, which upsets the fans, who complain that the clubs never spend money on players... Referees, meanwhile, do not please anyone.

Stakeholder analysis

The purpose of a stakeholder analysis is to identify stakeholders, their needs and relative influences. This enables the manager to satisfy these needs and/or deal with the influences in the most appropriate way.

A typical approach could be:

1 Identify the specific stakeholder groups.

2 Decide what they contribute to the organisation, that is, their function or connection to the organisation.

3 Specify what each stakeholder group wants from the organisation.

4 Consider the importance and influence of each stakeholder group on the performance of your organisation and rate each one as low, medium or high, where low is least important/influential.

5 Suggest how you can best meet the demands of the stakeholders – bearing in mind their importance/influence.

You could involve stakeholders themselves in this process by asking them, for example, what they expect from the organisation. This is something the California Energy Commission did in 1997 as part of its strategic plan.

The Energy Commission used internal and external inputs as part of its stakeholder analysis. Two approaches were used to gather external stakeholder input – focus groups and one-on-one interviews. A total of more than 40 organisations and 50 people participated. The primary goal of the focus groups and interviews was to get feedback on such questions as – What are the major challenges facing the energy industry of California? How might those challenges impact on the Energy Commission? What are your needs as customers of the Energy Commission? A survey was used for internal customers asking similar questions.

Source: *Adapted from California Energy Commission* (1997)

Although the California Energy Commission made a useful, comprehensive stakeholder analysis, an analysis of the industry as a whole would have been more instructive – as subsequent events have proven. The deregulation of the California electricity market in 1996 eventually led to chaos due to structural incompatibilities.

You could use a table to chart the results of a stakeholder analysis (see the activity below for an example). Of course, the fact that stakeholders want you to do something does not mean you have to do it. It is a question of priorities; for example, we would all like less taxes and higher wages, but...

Activity 8
Stakeholder analysis

Objective

This activity will help you to carry out a stakeholder analysis for your organisation.

Task

1 Complete the stakeholder chart for your work area/organisation.

2 Discuss your findings with your colleagues.

Chart for stakeholder analysis

My stakeholders	What they contribute	What they want	Importance and influence (1–5)	What I must do

Feedback

Here's an example of a simple stakeholder analysis conducted by the general manager of a local retailer.

My stakeholders	What they contribute	What they want	Importance and influence (1–5)	What I must do
Owner	Run the shop Order goods and supplies Accounting	Profits Well-run shop	5	Generate income Ensure the books are well managed
Employees	Operate the tills Stock movement	Wages and benefits Good working conditions	3	Pay minimum wage Provide same benefits for full and part-time staff Provide good working conditions
Suppliers	Provide products and supplies	Owner to buy their products Honour contracts	2	Meet representatives Pay within reasonable time
Customers	Buy products	Good products and service at the right price	3	Provide good customer service Keep prices keen
Regulatory bodies	Enforce health and safety, consumer protection regulations etc.	Compliance with rules and regulations Pay taxes	4	Follow rules and regulations Develop good relationships with regulators Pay taxes
Bank	Provide credit Provide accounts Give business advice	Interest on loans Well-managed accounts	4	Meet manager regularly Pay loans on time

Note that the importance and influence of any stakeholder may vary depending on who is doing the analysis, for example the suppliers might score themselves higher than 2. Also remember that circumstances might change and so increase the influence of a particular group.

Market analysis

The industry environment is the organisation's marketplace. It is where it buys and sells goods and services. Here we look at the economics of the industry environment, then focus on marketing analysis to assess your customers and potential customers so that you can effectively target them with your products and services.

Economics in the marketplace

Micro-economics is the behaviour of individual economic units, such as households and organisations, and their interaction in determining prices, supply and demand in market-based economies.

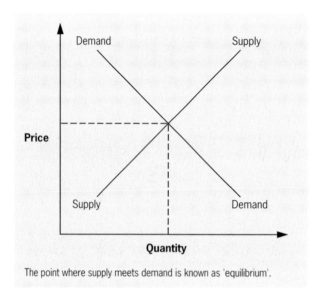

The point where supply meets demand is known as 'equilibrium'.

Figure 3.2 *Supply and demand*

The theory is simple enough. A market is an environment where buyers and sellers exchange goods and services. If there is more supply by organisations than demand by consumers, the price goes down. If there is more demand by consumers than supply by organisations, the price goes up – at least, in theory (see Figure 3.2). Stocks and shares, houses, petrol and coffee beans may act like this, but if your local supermarket is running out of beans, it is not going to put the price up just because there are only a few tins left. That would be counterproductive, as competition may induce the consumer to buy elsewhere next time or switch to mushy peas instead. The price of electricity does not go up just because there is more demand in winter. Mind you, that brings in a point about regulation. Governments will not keep out of the marketplace any more than they will keep out of anywhere else.

The important thing for government is not to do things which individuals are doing already, and to do them a little better or a little worse, but to do those things which at present are not done at all.

Source: *Keynes* (1926)

How does micro-economics affect me?

The market is what an organisation is about. It is where it sells its goods and services. You have even got an internal marketplace, of sorts – you have internal customers to whom you provide goods and services and internal suppliers who provide you with goods and services.

Managers need to be aware of the supply and demand factors in the organisation so that they can supply what customers demand at a price they want to pay.

Overpricing leads to cuts in demand; underpricing leads to loss of revenue. Having too many products when there is no demand puts up inventory and wastage costs. Not having enough products when there is a demand for them cuts profits. Hiring people too cheaply may bring the wrong level of skills. Hiring people too dearly may be overpaying for the value of the tasks they perform.

Over-supply, overestimation of demand and overestimation of the added value of new technology has created a worldwide market bubble (2000–2001). Though initially a tech bubble, it reaches out to all sectors because of the interdependence of the marketplace. Organisations are having to question the rationale of new technology in their own organisations when not so long ago any sort of technology was looked upon as giving them a competitive edge in their sector. For example, once it seemed everyone had to have knowledge management and its software. Suddenly it doesn't seem so important. UK knowledge management software company, Autonomy, the leader in the field, is feeling the pinch. Shares down from a high of £42 to £2.35 in five months (November 2000–April 2001). They didn't know it was coming.

So how do you get the balance right? What do you do? Here are some of the tasks managers might be involved in:

◆ making consumer and demographic profiles

◆ benchmarking industry prices

◆ assessing competitor products

- checking inventory

- assessing options on the capital market, for example bonds or shares

- assessing the state of the labour market – are there local skills shortages?

- forecasting product demand

- evaluating new technology as a value-driven factor

- negotiating agreements with suppliers – internal and external

- finding new sources of supply

- applying the marketing mix – planning all aspects of marketing a product or service to match the requirements of a specific market, such as price, product, promotion, place (the 4Ps).

A useful starting point is to learn about the market in which your organisation is operating.

Activity 9
The market economy

Objective

This activity focuses on the workings of the marketplace and will help you to assess how the marketplace works in terms of price, supply and demand.

Case study

As you read the case study, pay particular attention to what it says about supply and demand and prices.

> **Beyond the pool; Electricity markets; Britain's electricity gamble**
>
> Could Britain's electricity market be going the way of California's? It may seem an outlandish question, given that Britain led the world in liberalising its power industry a decade ago – and so successfully that it has inspired reformers everywhere. California tried to copy Britain, but mucked things up badly. The state's utilities are bankrupt and consumers are enduring blackouts. The governor is even now organising a bail-out for those utilities, which owe creditors more than $10 billion, by offering to buy their transmission assets at inflated prices.
>
> The key blunder in the California 'deregulation' was setting free the wholesale market for power while keeping prices fixed in the retail

market. When the price of the power that the utilities were forced to buy unexpectedly soared, they found they could not pass on the extra costs to consumers. This squeeze has been made worse by the lack of 'real-time' metering: users receive no price signals when demand peaks – and so have no incentive to conserve.

Some analysts are suggesting that upcoming changes to Britain's electricity regulations will tinker with a successful model in ways that are reminiscent of, albeit not identical to, these mistakes. Generators are currently required to sell their output through a central pool in which distributors bid every half-hour. The system is reliable, but has some unnecessary costs, since the highest bid required to ensure that supply matches demand sets the price for all the power sold in that session. What is more, the government found that some operators were manipulating the system and inflating prices. So it has decided to scrap the pool and move to a market-based system for wholesale power known as the New Electricity Trading Arrangements (NETA). Under the new system, which is due to start on March 27th, generators will be free to contract directly with purchasers.

Will it work? Dieter Helm of Oxford Economic Research Associates, a consultancy, argues that NETA may actually end up stifling competition, just as Britain's electricity business consolidates into fewer integrated firms. (This week, for instance, Innogy, a big generator, bought Yorkshire Power, a distribution firm, for over $2.5 billion.) Mr Helm worries that 'NETA may actually reduce the threat of entry' because the lack of a mandatory pool will force new entrants into the wholesale market to buy power direct from incumbents that also happen to be their rivals.

Even if the sceptics are proven wrong and the system does deliver lower prices, it is still likely to increase price volatility in the short term. One reason is that the complex new system may suffer teething pains; already, technical glitches have delayed things once. In recent days, some jittery electricity firms have grumbled that the government should delay the launch by a few months. Officials this week insisted that NETA will start as planned, but traders say a cloud of uncertainty hangs over the market.

Britain will surely survive these bumps in better shape than California, but it may yet run into problems in the longer term. Schroder Salomon Smith Barney (SSSB), an investment bank, warns – with Britain in mind – that 'in certain situations, the Californian scenario could be repeated, especially if exacerbated by ill-judged or regulatory intervention.'

Defenders of NETA point out that California set wholesale prices free in a market with tight supply, while Britain today has excess capacity. That is true, but as SSSB's Anthony White notes, the British retail market is fragmented and competitive: this means that firms will find it hard to pass on any increase in wholesale costs to customers. This is especially true if, as officials predict, NETA squeezes out the 10% or so of 'excess' profits that generators are supposedly pocketing today. Eroding margins will make it unattractive to build plants, and spare capacity will eventually decline – as in California.

In a properly deregulated market, this would not be a problem: wholesale supply crunches would lead to higher retail prices, which would curb demand and provide incentives for new capacity. There's the rub: retail electricity prices in Britain, as in California, are not free to fluctuate with demand. Except for a few heavy users, real-time metering does not exist. Most residential meters in Britain are read only sporadically, yet the cost of power varies all the time. This suggests a flawed market design.

In a new book, 'Competition in Electricity Markets', the International Energy Agency argues that 'approaches that do not fully deregulate generation and end-user supply are not sustainable ... partial market opening is likely to distort prices.' The agency's boffins say price signals are essential, even if only through simple meters that alert customers when demand is at its peak. In parts of Europe, 'red light/green light' meters already do the trick.

Does metering really matter this much? A new study by the Electric Power Research Institute (EPRI), a research body linked to America's utilities, analysed the effect sophisticated metering had in tests in the south-eastern United States and in Britain's Midlands. It concluded that real-time pricing applied to just a portion of California's industrial customers could reduce peak demand by about 2.5%. This makes the biggest difference when capacity is tightest, says EPRI 's Ahmad Faruqui: when a power shortage looms, a drop in demand of only 2.5% reduces wholesale prices by up to 24%. Britain's regulators would do well to start selling the industry and the public on the notion of real-time metering now, before that theoretical supply crunch becomes reality.

Source: *The Economist* (2001)

Task

1 List some key points on how problems with supply, demand and prices in the California/UK electricity industry can adversely affect utilities working in these markets.

Key points:

Feedback

Here are some key points that you may have included in your list:

◆ California set wholesale prices free in a market with tight supply, while keeping prices fixed in a retail market with heavy demand. When the wholesale price went up, utilities couldn't pass on the costs.

◆ In the US, users receive no price signals when demand peaks and so have no incentive to conserve.

♦ The UK central pool system has some unnecessary costs, since the highest bid required to ensure that supply matches demand sets the price for all the power sold in that session.

♦ The UK system has excess supply, unlike California, but the NETA system could squeeze margins because, as in California, prices are not free to fluctuate with demand.

The International Energy Agency argues that 'approaches that do not fully deregulate generation and end-user supply are not sustainable ... partial market opening is likely to distort prices.' They say price signals are essential, even if only through simple meters that alert customers when demand is at its peak.

Market research

Market research is a systematic collection and analysis of data about your target market, competition and/or environment. Its purpose is to:

♦ identify product opportunities in the marketplace

♦ identify potential problems with current marketing

♦ find out about your customers, their habits and likes/dislikes, their expectations, needs and wants

♦ identify your competitors and their strengths and weaknesses

♦ help you develop a marketing plan

♦ help measure success.

There are many ways to carry out market research, such as:

♦ customer feedback surveys

♦ desk/computer research

♦ focus groups

♦ questionnaires.

Electronic surveys are quite useful as they can quickly reach a wide audience. They are easy to collate with a back-end database. Here is an e-example from the Education Marketplace – www.education-net.co.uk.

Online market research survey – We value your opinion

In order that we continue to meet the needs of our market, we are conducting an ongoing market research survey on this site. The first part of this survey can be seen below. **Completing the questionnaire.** Answer the questions listed below. Your answers will then be forwarded to us. If you select "Other" at any point in the questionnaire, we will contact you directly to discuss your needs.

Visitor questions

1	Do you use the Internet before purchasing?	○ Yes	○ No
2	Do you/would you buy online?	○ Yes	○ No

2a **If yes, what range of products?**

Books	○ Yes	○ No
Art materials	○ Yes	○ No
Science materials	○ Yes	○ No
Software	○ Yes	○ No
Other	○ Yes	○ No

2b **If no, why not?**

Security	○ Yes	○ No
No credit card facilities at school	○ Yes	○ No
No purchasing power	○ Yes	○ No

3 **What areas of the website have you found most useful?**

Case studies	○
Market research	○
Bett 2001	○
Education show 2001	○

4 **What other information could we provide?**

An online shopping facility	○ Yes	○ No
An Ask The Expert section	○ Yes	○ No
An online chat room	○ Yes	○ No
A choice of European languages to read the site	○ Yes	○ No

Your name: [   ]

Email: [   ]

[Submit]

Figure 3.3 *E-survey*   Source: *Education Marketplace* (www)

Activity 10
Market research

Objective

For this activity you need to find out about market research in your organisation. Use the activity to identify the purpose and nature of market research used by your organisation and how it aids decision making.

Task

1 Find out what market research your organisation carries out. Which of the following has it recently used?

  ☐ desk/computer research to analyse existing data

  ☐ customer surveys – collecting data first hand from customers

  ☐ focus groups to find out the feelings and opinions of typical members of a target market.

2 What is the purpose of market research? Tick the relevant boxes in the list below:

  ☐ to identify product opportunities in the marketplace

  ☐ to find out who your customers are and what their habits and likes/dislikes are

  ☐ to identify competitors and their strengths and weaknesses

  ☐ to help in developing a marketing plan

  ☐ to identify potential problems with current marketing

  ☐ to help measure success.

3 How could you use market research in your department/work area to get the views of your internal customers?

Using market research:

Feedback

Much of the information gathered by organisations can be used to understand what customers want. Sales figures and data about customer complaints, for example, can both give information about customers. Your organisation may draw on information gathered and published by third parties, for example the government, that examines consumer trends. Trade journals often give marketing information. You may find that your organisation commissions market research specialists to conduct research on its behalf, or it may have sufficient resources to conduct its own research.

To find out about the views of your internal customers – the people who receive the products and services your department provides – you could write a simple questionnaire and ask them to complete it. You could also get together informally with these internal customers and ask them for their views. You can use this information to plan ways of better meeting their needs.

The Ansoff matrix

After you have conducted your market research, how do you then make the most of the markets available to you? Igor Ansoff devised a strategic marketing tool in the 1950s to help identify possible opportunities in the marketplace (Ansoff, 1966). It is widely known as the product-market matrix or the Ansoff matrix and consists of four strategic choices:

1 Using an **existing market** to promote an **existing product**. This suggests market penetration.

2 Finding a **new market** to promote an **existing product**. This suggests market development.

3 Using an **existing market** for a **new product**. This suggests product development.

4 Finding a **new market** for a **new product**. This suggests diversification.

We will look at each in turn.

1 Market penetration

Using an existing market for an existing product is a fairly conservative marketing strategy. You can:

◆ concentrate on your core markets and try to consolidate

◆ increase market share

◆ retrench or sell out – that is, decide to get out to cut costs and/or concentrate on core activities.

For example, the personal computer (PC) market worldwide is dominated by about five companies, such as IBM, Dell and Compaq, which have successfully managed to consolidate their positions over the years. This has resulted in others, such as Amstrad in the UK, getting out of the market to concentrate on other products and markets.

2 Market development

Another marketing strategy is to use existing products but find new markets for them.

- This could be by finding new market segments, such as targeting pensions at children (in the UK, legislation in 2001 enables parents to take out low-cost stakeholder pensions for their children)

- It could be finding new geographical areas such as exporting satellite TV to Mongol herdsmen.

3 Product development

This strategy is to use new products in existing markets, such as supermarkets which target their customers with financial services. Alternatively, you may extend the range and life of a product by:

- dressing up the same product in a different way, for example, new improved Persil washing powder, new model Ford Mondeo cars

- product diversification – this means you extend the range of the product, for example, making soft drinks alcoholic or making ice creams from confectionery like Mars bars.

4 Diversification

This seems the most risky market strategy – finding new markets for new products – although at least you do not have all your eggs in one basket.

> Starting off with Virgin Records, Richard Branson has diversified into a whole range of new products and markets with his Virgin group – trains, planes, radio, holidays, cola, energy, lightships, wines, books, mobiles, bridal emporiums, cars, financial services, Web hosting, cosmetics, student services, balloons, etc. You may like to check out www.virgin.com for the full set.

It should be noted that organisations may use mixes of these four strategies at the same time depending on the range of their products and markets. This would certainly be the case with the Virgin Group.

Activity 11
The Ansoff matrix

Objective

Use this activity to apply the Ansoff matrix to organisations.

Task

1 Apply the Ansoff matrix approach to different organisations (including your own if you wish) by listing two examples for each of the matrix categories using the table below. There is an example provided.

2 Explain the benefits and risks of each of the four approaches.

	Existing products	New products
Existing markets	1 **Market penetration** Tesco increasing its share of the food retailing market Vodaphone selling Orange	3 **Product development** Tesco offering Internet shopping Banks offering flexible mortgages
New markets	2 **Market development** Tesco expanding into Europe (35% of its group sales) Inland revenue taxing contractors as employees (IR35)	4 **Diversification** Virgin Group moving into trips on lightships Tesco selling cars

	Existing products	New products
Existing markets	1 **Market penetration**	3 **Product development**
New markets	2 **Market development**	4 **Diversification**

Source: *Ansoff* (1966)

65

Benefits and risks:

Feedback

1 Share your examples with colleagues to see what they came up with.

2 **Market penetration** means that you are focusing on your core activities, the ones you do best, though as markets grow or shrink this can produce problems as it means all your eggs are in one basket.

Market development is a more dynamic strategy as you are going for growth, but you could waste time and money in a market that 'won't take', for example trillions of dollars were lost in the Russian market in the 1980s.

Product development moves away from your normal, core activity; it is a growth strategy and so can pay dividends. However, product development implies high costs in research and development and there have been spectacular product failures, for example the Robin Reliant.

Diversification is the riskiest strategy – a lot of different eggs in different baskets. It may be a good hedging strategy, but you can become overstretched. For example, do you think Virgin may be overstretched?

Industry analysis

Industry analysis focuses on the competitive situation within an industry. Here we look at two approaches to industry analysis – the Five Force model and benchmarking.

The challenge

Industry analysis is particularly useful where technological and structural change is so commonplace, especially in 21st century markets (as the next case study shows).

Phillip Townsend Associates Predicts Dramatic Changes in the Thermoplastics Distribution Industry

A new study, 'Thermoplastics Distributors and Resellers, North America: Industry Analysis, Company Strategies and Profiles,' by Phillip Townsend Associates (Townsend) is scheduled for release during the 4th quarter of 2001. This new study will provide detailed information and actionable insights into the distributor and reseller industry.

Kevin Smith, project manager for the study, said, 'The study will concentrate on the industry as it exists in 2001 and how it will evolve over the next five years.' As of the most recent data, Townsend estimates that the distributor and reseller market in North America represents over 3.5 billion pounds of resin sales. These resins were then sold to an estimated 4,000 converting sites in North America.

Townsend is forecasting change in this market. According to Smith, 'This change will be as a result of consolidation of producers. The creation of e-businesses by the resin producers is changing and the consolidation of distribution channels will have an impact on the conventional distribution channels as we know them today.'

In conjunction with this study, Townsend will provide a unique picture of the alliance between resin producers and distributors. The study will describe, in detail, the distribution market in 2001 and the forecast for 2006.

'However,' Smith says, 'our experience is that the secondary distribution channels are poorly characterized. That is a primary reason for doing the study – to better define the secondary distribution channels.'

This study will be recommended reading for all resin producers, distributors and e-businesses supplying the polymer industry.

Source: *Business Wire* (2001a)

The Five Force model

The Five Force model was developed by Professor Michael Porter, a US writer on strategy, in the late 1970s. It is an industry analysis tool which seeks to evaluate the competitive situation within an industry.

The model is based on the strength of five forces which act on an industry – see Figure 3.4.

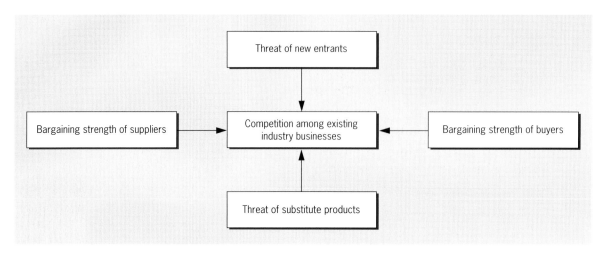

Figure 3.4 *Porter's Five Force model*   Source: *Adapted from Porter* (1980)

The forces can be explained as follows:

◆ **Bargaining strength of suppliers.** Are suppliers many and competitive, or few, perhaps because they have a monopoly or a unique product? For example, few can match Microsoft's Windows architecture and this puts the company in a strong position. Strong suppliers can keep prices high.

◆ **Threat of new entrants.** Is competition likely to increase or decrease? Are there barriers to entry such as capital outlay or regulation? Is entry easy through deregulation? Consider how many companies have diversified into financial services over the last few years. On the other hand, Railtrack has monopoly control of the railway infrastructure with no one threatening its position.

◆ **Bargaining strength of buyers.** For example, supermarkets in the UK buy from farmers. There are about six major supermarket companies, and numerous farmers. These farmers complain that the supermarket companies have a near-monopolistic control over them, forcing them to trim margins despite the poor financial state of the agriculture industry.

◆ **Threat of substitute products.** For example, MP3, a new digital music product, is threatening to dislodge traditional music products and outlets from their markets. Other examples include the growth of own-brand labels in supermarkets, vegetarian alternatives to meat, LPG as an alternative to petrol, etc. Substitutes can drive prices down.

◆ **Competition among existing industry businesses.** What is the current level of competition? Is there a cartel like OPEC? Are competitors vibrant and innovative as in high-tech industries? Is competition regulated as in the power and energy industry? Is there high or low growth? Are margins tight? Are there many or few competitors?

A Five Force model of the music recording/publishing industry could focus on these points:

◆ Bargaining strength of suppliers – there are many artists and few last the course; they are dependent on larger recording companies' power, say, for marketing. However, with new PC technology, artists are able to publish their work without recording companies.

◆ Threat of new entrants – artists can set up their own record companies or produce recordings cheaply on the Net; new companies come and go quite often; Web-based companies have sprung up (for example Napster, which pioneered free MP3).

◆ Bargaining strength of buyers – music shops are dependent on recording companies but customers (secondary buyers) of the shops are not, for example, music on the radio, Net, TV – shops are in a weak position.

◆ Threat of substitute products – MP3, free music files on the Internet, pirate recordings.

◆ Competition among existing industry businesses – fierce as tight margins force mergers (for example, EMI acquiring 51 per cent stake in Hit & Run Music Publishing); industry making alliances with Net software companies such as AOL Time Warner, Bertelsmann and EMI with RealNetworks.

Conclusion

The industry alliances, particularly record companies with Net companies, and the legal action against organisations such as Napster which used copyrighted material, put the record companies in a strong position to regain any ground they have lost and indeed strengthen their hold in the market.

Activity 12
Industry analysis

Objective

This activity will help you to analyse the competitive nature of your industry. It asks you to carry out a Five Force analysis of your industry.

Task

1   Make a Five Force analysis of your own industry using the five categories. Work with your colleagues on this if you wish.

Bargaining strength of suppliers

Bargaining strength of buyers

Threat of new entrants

Threat of substitute products

Competition among existing industry businesses

2 Draw some conclusions about the state of your industry. Where are the key competitive pressures in your industry? For example, suppliers may have a strong bargaining position and be able to set prices, or buyers may have a wide choice and may easily be able to switch between one organisation's products and another's. What is your organisation's position within this industry and what are the implications for its strategy?

Feedback

Have a look back at the examples in this section and compare your model with the explanations there. Discuss the state of your industry and your organisation's position within it with your colleagues.

Benchmarking

Benchmarking is a tool to help improve performance by looking outside the organisation at other organisations' best practices, systems, technologies and business processes. It started off as a way of analysing best practice in an industry, but can have much wider (or narrower) applications.

Countries can benchmark other countries; organisations benchmark other organisations which they admire; public-sector organisations benchmark other public-sector organisations; e-businesses benchmark other e-businesses. Also, one part of an organisation may benchmark its practices against another part of the same organisation.

Benchmarking involves four basic steps:

1 Examine your own practices and processes.

2 Analyse the practices and processes of organisations that are ahead in your sector. What are the benefits of these practices?

3 Identify areas where improvements can be made through adoption or adaptation of others' best practices and processes – these are the 'benchmarks'.

4 Develop and implement a plan to utilise benchmarks to close the performance gap.

To be effective, benchmarking should be ongoing, so it can also be used as a monitoring and control tool.

A benchmarking of best practices in using the Web for the US healthcare industry found that:

♦ research could be conducted quicker and more efficiently, increasing the speed of medical intervention and reducing costs

♦ online communications enhanced productivity

♦ online data such as billing could be processed quicker

♦ online links with pharmacists regarding prescriptions achieved productivity improvements for both parties

♦ tailored services via the Internet, such as crisis management, patient support and information provision, reduced industry risk

♦ by combining many services, programs and features into as few applications as possible, there were cost savings in staff training, system maintenance and program portability and synergy

♦ formalised documentation improved record keeping and position for potential audits.

Source: *Adapted from Global Benchmarking Council* (1999)

There are a number of good websites about benchmarking with plenty of examples of how it is done. See the 'More @' section at the end of this theme.

♦ Recap

This theme provides tools and techniques to support analyis of the organisational environment.

Carry out a stakeholder analysis for your organisation

♦ Stakeholders are those people and groups who are affected by and affect the performance of the organisation.

♦ The purpose of stakeholder analysis is to identify stakeholders, their needs and their relative influences.

Assess how the marketplace works in terms of price, supply and demand

♦ Managers need to be aware of the supply and demand factors in the organisation so that they can supply what customers demand at a price they want to pay.

Identify the purpose and nature of market research used by your organisation and how it aids decision making

◆ Market research can be used to:

- identify product opportunities

- identify potential problems with marketing

- find out about customers

- identify competitors

- help devise a marketing plan

- measure success.

Apply the Ansoff matrix to identify possible opportunities in the market

◆ Ansoff devised a strategic marketing tool to help identify possible opportunities in the marketplace.

◆ The strategic choices are:

- market penetration

- market development

- product development

- diversification.

Analyse the competitive nature of your industry and carry out a Five Force analysis

◆ Porter's Five Force model seeks to evaluate the competitive situation within an industry. The forces are:

- bargaining strength of suppliers

- threat of new entrants

- bargaining strength of buyers

- threat of substitute products

- competition among existing industry businesses.

Consider benchmarking as an industry analysis tool

◆ Benchmarking is a tool to help improve performance by looking outside the organisation at best practices, systems, technologies and business processes.

◆ Benchmarking involves examining your own practices, analysing the practices of the organisations that are ahead in the sector, identifying areas for improvement and developing plans to close the performance gap.

More @

Campbell, D., Stonehouse, G. and Houston, B. (2002) 2nd edition, *Business Strategy: an Introduction*, Elsevier Butterworth-Heinemann
This is an accessible textbook that provides a straightforward and comprehensive guide to complex issues and concepts. See Chapter 7 'Analysis of the competitive environment' and Chapter 8 'Competitive advantage: strategies, knowledge and core competences'.

Porter, M. E. (1980) *Competitive Strategy: Techniques for Analysing Industries and Competitors*, The Free Press
Porter shows how competitive advantage can be defined in terms of relative cost and relative prices, thus linking it directly to profitability, and presents a whole new perspective on how profit is created and divided.

Diversification – www.virgin.com
Look at the website for the Virgin group (www.virgin.com) to find out more about diversification.

Benchmarking

There are a number of good websites about benchmarking with plenty of examples of how it's done:

www.benchmarking.co.uk – The Benchmarking Centre, free registration

www.benchmarking-in-europe.com – Global Benchmarking Council, a European Commission site for promoting benchmarking in Europe

www.globalbenchmarking.com – a site which creates reports from benchmarking exercises, and has a best practices database. It is a commercial site, but there is still plenty of free information.

You could also have a look at the magazine *Benchmarking: An International Journal* published by MCB University Press – www.mcb.co.uk/bij.htm.

Full references are provided at the end of the book.

4 The macro environment

The macro environment spans politics, economics, social matters, technology, legislation and eco-environmental factors. This series of readings and activities reviews each of these factors to help you assess their impact on your organisation.

Here are just a few of the issues we face:

If only organisations could go about doing what they were good at, without interference from government.	V	Doesn't the government have a duty to act on our behalf to provide social protection?
Think about how your organisation tries to balance spending, investment and debt.	V	Consider how your organisation is affected by macro-economic factors like interest rates, currency prices, consumption and fiscal policy.
We want to be a socially responsible organisation and act to the positive advantage of our community.	V	We have to be aware of the economic consequences of any decisions we make.
Technology has moved civilisation from straw hats and oxen to virtual reality and TGVs.	V	We are all at the mercy of the dehumanising effects of new technologies.
Employment and corporate law provides protection for the health, safety and welfare of our employees.	V	Employment, consumer and corporate law places a heavy economic, ethical and social burden on the employer.
Our business is keen to understand consumers' perceptions of our impact on the eco-environment.	V	There are many other stakeholders with a vested interest when it comes to the eco-environment.

This theme concludes with a PESTLE analysis – the quintessential analysis tool for assessing factors in the external environment. PESTLE stands for **P**olitical, **E**conomic, **S**ocial, **T**echnological, **L**egislative/legal, **E**co-environmental.

Within this theme you will:

◆ **Evaluate the impact of political factors on organisations**

◆ **Define some key economic terms and assess the impact of European Monetary Union on your organisation**

◆ **Examine social trends and explore a demographic profile to assess its implications for organisations**

◆ **Consider the organisational impact of new technologies**

◆ **See how three types of legislation impact on three different stakeholders: employment law (employees), consumer law (customers) and corporate law (owners)**

◆ **Carry out an eco-environmental audit of your organisation or work area**

◆ **Carry out a PESTLE analysis.**

The macro environment: politics

One of the bugbears of the modern organisation is political interference. If only organisations could go about doing what they are good at without this interference, how much more productive and efficient they would be. But would there be more Robert Maxwells? Less synergy with stakeholders? More exploitation? Does the government not have a duty to act on our behalf to provide social protection?

This is the first of six reviews of factors in the macro environment.

Local and national

Sometimes it is not easy to distinguish the political from the economic.

Politicians love spending other people's money – wouldn't you? – and this, of course, includes the organisation's money.

The question for governments seems to be not so much 'how much?' as 'how many ways are there to do it?'

At the local level, businesses have to pay non-domestic rates, more colloquially known as business rates. The non-domestic rate income is paid into a national pool and then redistributed between local authorities in proportion to their adult population. Business rates fund about one third of councils' spending.

More interesting is tax at national level, which includes:

◆ corporation tax (on profits)

◆ national insurance

◆ VAT (reclaimable but, oh, the paperwork!)

◆ social security taxes such as statutory sick pay and statutory maternity pay.

There is a host of other taxes, such as landfill tax, stamp duty and a possible future energy tax. And if you live in Scotland, watch out for extra taxes from the national assembly.

Try www.inlandrevenue.gov.uk if you want to know more.

It is not just taxes, though. It is also the cost of administering government initiatives such as tax, health and safety legislation, stakeholder pensions, family friendly policies, statutory sick pay (SSP) and statutory maternity pay (SMP) etc. Not that the government is unaware of the burden. There are always allowances made.

Not all political impacts mean costs for the organisation!
In the UK budget for 2001, Gordon Brown, the Chancellor, unveiled a host of plans to help small and medium-sized enterprises (SMEs). These included:

◆ consultation on a radical new look at the tax treatment of small businesses aimed at reducing regulatory burdens through aligning their profits for tax purposes broadly with those reported in their accounts

◆ measures to manage SMEs' entry into the VAT system, reduce burdens and improve their cash flow – such as greater availability of the cash and annual accounting schemes and consultation on the flat rate and annual accounting schemes

◆ improvements to Enterprise Management Incentives (EMI) to make it easier for companies to operate – such as removing the limit on the number of employees in each company who can hold EMI options, doubling the limit on the total value of shares under EMI options to £3 million, and offering advance assurance on whether or not a company qualifies

◆ consultation on proposals to change the rules for life insurance companies that invest in venture capital limited partnerships

◆ relaxing some of the rules of the Enterprise Investment Scheme, Venture Capital Trust Scheme and Corporate Venturing Scheme to make it easier for small entrepreneurial companies to raise equity and long-term finance.

Note the use of the word 'consultation' here. You will come back to this point later on.

EU and global

Political impacts on organisations are not just at local and national levels. Increasingly, European Union and global factors are making an impact.

Consider the following.

'Daft' EU Flowerpot Ruling Upheld
The horticultural industry today reacted with disappointment to a High Court ruling that plastic flowerpots amounted to 'packaging' under a European Union directive aimed at reclaiming and recycling waste material. The decision means that UK growers may have to pay for the plastic pots to be recovered and recycled. They say they will now be put at a

disadvantage by a directive that the rest of Europe ignores or interprets differently and which an MP says leaves European Commissioners looking like Bill and Ben the flowerpot men. Legal experts say the decision, by Lord Woolf, the Lord Chief Justice, and Mr Justice Newman, could also affect many other types of business.

In a test case which left Euro-sceptics fuming, the judges decided that Hillier Nurseries Ltd, based at Romsey, Hampshire, in 1998 had breached the Producer Responsibility Obligations (Packaging Waste) Regulations by not including plastic flower pots in their calculations of waste packaging. The regulations required companies with a turnover of £5 million, now reduced to £2 million, and producing packaging exceeding 50 tonnes to pay for a proportion of the waste to be collected and recycled. The court refused permission to appeal and decided that the case should not be referred to the European Court of Justice.

Sir Teddy Taylor, Conservative MP for Rochford and Southend East, said the ruling demonstrated 'how daft and irresponsible European directives are becoming and interfering in every aspect of our way of life'.

Source: *The Times* (2001)

The debate on the European Union is not too different from the debate about government's role at national and local level. Governments argue that they interfere for social, economic and environmental reasons – to smooth out injustices, discrepancies and other effects arising from the chaos of millions of individuals interacting with each other. But how far do they actually contribute to the very 'diseases' they are trying to 'cure'?

The European Union proceeds by treaties – Single European Act, the Maastricht Treaty, the Amsterdam Treaty, the Treaty of Nice – and directives drawn up by the Council of Ministers and European Commission (EC). The EC is unelected and is frequently under pressure to reform. Its en masse resignation in March 1999 after allegations of fraud and corruption did nothing to dispel the fear that government from afar is too far.

If you want to know more about the EU, EC and their workings, you could check out www.cec.org.uk/index.htm – the website of the European Commission representation in the UK. For more about EU issues which affect organisations, you could search the archives of The Times at www.thetimes.co.uk.

On the global front, the G7/G8 meetings of the US, Japan, Germany, France, the UK, Italy and Canada (and Russia) provide a focus for global political matters. Although originally a vehicle for discussions of world macro-economic and monetary policy, international trade, debt and development, etc., this has now expanded to cover issues such as the environment, drugs, education, foreign policy and nuclear power. Foreign ministers and finance ministers usually meet separately from prime ministers. Policies shaped and negotiated in G7 summits can affect the trading environment, business competitiveness and the quality of life of people all over the world. Many of the commitments may be just promises, but many filter through to organisations eventually as extra commitments, taxes, duties and attitudes. This is particularly true of environmental issues, for example in the 1990s and early 2000s.

Managing politics

Russian Metals Execs Mastering Politics

MOSCOW – When Alexander Khloponin, head of the world's biggest palladium producer and second-biggest nickel producer, was elected governor of Taimyr, the 35-year-old company director joined a growing number of Russia's business elite who are moving into politics...

'Khloponin's win is the culmination of a two-year drive for political power in Taimyr,' said Mikhail Malyutin of the Expert Institute of the Russian Union of Industrialists and Entrepreneurs – dubbed the 'trade union of the oligarchs'. Last year, he said, 'the company helped get its candidates elected to the local Duma and supported the winner in mayoral elections in Norilsk'...

In Russian politics there is no such thing as a norm against conflict of interest. If there were, the corridors of power would be empty...

... the new governor will be using his new powers to lobby for his company, and new legislation may allow him to do this for many years to come. Few voices are likely to be heard in opposition. 'There is nothing unusual in a company's wish to control the regions that are their main field of operation,' said Alexel Titkov, a regional policy analyst at Moscow Carnegie Center. 'It's a fact of life'...

In a region like Taimyr, where there is only one employer, it is in the interests of both the company and the population to cooperate, he added.

Source: *Forster* (2001)

Russia has a rather different interpretation of a liberal democracy than most of the West. But consultation with government and lobbying are key aspects of any informal democratic process. Lobbying can work at all levels: EU, parliamentary, regional and local government.

There was an outbreak of foot-and-mouth disease in the UK in early 2001. The UK government, in response to pleas for financial help from companies in trouble as a result of the knock-on effects of the outbreak, extended their Small Firms Loan Guarantee Scheme to a wider range of companies such as garages, restaurants and souvenir shops. Repayment periods were also extended.

You can also lobby the G7 as there are sometimes business conferences going on at the same time as their meetings. Lobbying is about:

◆ communicating with individual politicians

◆ communicating with government departments

◆ developing formal or informal contacts with civil servants

◆ using professional lobbyists

◆ taking part in democratic forums and local meetings with politicians and others, for example for approval of local plans

◆ taking part in commercial/government conferences and seminars

◆ using media influence, for example issuing press releases and policy statements, sending e-mails

◆ taking direct action, for example the 'petrol protest' by lorry driver-owners in autumn 2000 in the UK and parts of Europe.

By lobbying and consultation, organisations can bring issues which will affect them to the attention of politicians, and get the politicians to alter their courses of action. In addition, by anticipating the impact of political events such as the impact of taxes and legislation, organisations can budget and organise accordingly and avoid the penalties of non-compliance.

The macro environment: economics

Here we look at economics and how it affects organisations at the macro level.

Key terminology

Macro-economics covers the larger economic trends such as the national economy, government economic policy, unemployment, trade and globalisation.

Table 4.1 gives some of the key concepts in macro-economics.

Macro-economic concepts	What they mean
Gross domestic product (GDP)	The value of all the products and services a country sells internally and externally
Consumption	The amount we spend
Savings and investments	Unspent income, usually deposited at a bank for a fixed interest rate, and unspent income used to produce capital gain
National debt	The sum of all unremitted government borrowing
Inflation	Increase in prices and fall in the purchasing power of money
Trade gap/balance of payments	The difference between the value of imports and exports, including capital imports/exports
Growth rate	The speed at which the economy is rising in value
Monetary policy	Decreasing/increasing money in the economy to curb/encourage spending, often by altering bank interest rates
Fiscal policy	Taxation as a way of raising public money and dealing with the economy

Table 4.1 *Macro-economic concepts*

Capitalist economies exist on debt. The government, organisations and private individuals leverage their wealth by borrowing. The debt can be sustained as long as the borrower repays the interest. By the time the capital is repaid, if at all, enough money should have been made to pay off the debt.

Debt is a double-edged sword. In boom times, debt is cheap and this encourages growth. But if there is too much money available, that is, the market is too 'liquid', this can encourage uncontrolled investment and inflation. A downturn may then occur as supply outstrips demand. This is then self-perpetuating, as debt is called in, interest rates go up and businesses fail – the so-called 'economic cycle'.

The 'new economy' is a 1990s paradigm of sustained economic growth based on technology. The belief is that technology creates real productivity gains which, coupled with high employment, low interest rates, sustainable debt and low inflation – an unheard of number of plus factors at the same time – produces an expanding, boom-and-bust-free economy. Sceptics suggested that the inflationary level of stock-market prices (particularly in technology), highly leveraged debt – in 2001 global debt was $90,000 billion, 300 per cent of world GDP – and over-liquidity would eventually bring the whole world economy crashing down.

Think about how your organisation tries to balance spending, investment and debt, and how it is affected by macro-economic factors like interest rates, currency prices, consumption and fiscal policy.

Globalisation

The deregulation of financial markets, advance of information technology, lowering of trade barriers based on the work of the World Trade Organisation (WTO), retreat of communism and development of multinational organisations has led to a phenomenon known as globalisation.

This means that events in one place can quickly affect events in another. For example, the defaulting of Russia on its debt in 1998 sent world stock markets into a spin. It could mean your local water or electricity company is owned by a French or German company. It could mean you could locate parts of your organisation to somewhere where goods are made more cheaply – a common practice in car manufacturing. It could mean you are a 24-hour organisation operating in many different time zones at once.

> The Internet-routing gear company, Cisco Systems, only has three manufacturing plants of its own. The other 30 or so are contract manufacturers. They are worldwide and connected to Cisco by an extranet. When Cisco gets an order, the contract manufacturers compete for the contract based on price, quality and delivery time.

How is your organisation affected by globalisation?

Back to politics again

Macro-economic events are also political. Monetary policy, fiscal policy, inflation, consumer spending and employment are all concerns of governments and ones they feel free to influence. Think about the minimum wage, family friendly policies, employment legislation, direct and indirect taxes, or the way currency rates affect manufacturing exports. Governments touch the organisation and affect it in a million and one ways.

> As part of the EU, the UK is affected by its economic policies. Economic and Monetary Union (EMU) is a huge issue for organisations, not least in the planning and budgeting to implement it should it ever arrive. It means changing all your in-house vending machines for a start! Exporters and multinationals point to the savings that will be made on currency conversion charges. Others point out that centralising monetary policy and interest rates will take away a key economic tool that enables national economies to control their economies. The only alternative would be to use fiscal policy – not to everyone's taste. And if fiscal policy gets harmonised next, what about sovereignty?

Activity 13
Politics and economics

Objective

In this activity you will consider macro-economics in terms of political involvement. It will help you to assess the impact of the macro-economic environment on organisations.

One particular politico-economic factor which is likely to have a huge effect on organisations is Economic and Monetary Union (EMU). EMU is aimed at harmonising economic/monetary activities in the EU by the adoption of a single currency – the euro. This was implemented in January 2002 amongst the majority of EU countries. The Central European Bank in Frankfurt sets interest rates for participating members. The effects of entering EMU are considered to be good or bad depending on who you listen to.

Task

You can use external resources to help you with this activity, such as www.emuaware.forfas.ie. You will find plenty of help if you search the Internet under 'economic and monetary union' or 'EMU'.

1   Draw up a list of five or six pros and cons of the UK entering EMU from **the organisational viewpoint**.

2   Discuss what you think is the right decision for your organisation with your colleagues.

Pros of EMU for organisations	Cons of EMU for organisations

Feedback

Some of the pros and cons of EMU for organisations are listed below:

Pros of EMU for organisations	Cons of EMU for organisations
◆ No transaction charges for imported goods	◆ Changeover costs for: pricing; finance and accounting systems, sales and purchasing administration, payroll and pension systems, software systems; company vending machines; documentation; training
◆ No fluctuations in exchange rates between EU members, for example, a high £ adversely affects manufacturers	◆ Fluctuations against the $ will still produce ups and downs
◆ One interest rate means a level playing field for borrowing	◆ Higher corporate taxes as fiscal policy becomes the major UK economic tool
◆ One interest rate means a level playing field for competition	◆ UK organisations may lose competitiveness as a result of levelling of EU tax rates
◆ Transparency and harmonisation in EU prices and wages	◆ Harmonisation of prices/wages inappropriate except for pan-European organisations

Whether entering EMU is a good thing or a bad thing is a matter of personal opinion and depends on the particular positioning of your organisation.

The macro environment: social matters

> 'No one would remember the Good Samaritan if he'd only had good intentions. He had money as well.'
>
> **Margaret Thatcher, Television interview, 6 January, 1986**

Social matters cover a number of different areas in the business environment, such as social trends, stakeholders, social responsibility and business ethics.

Social trends

Social trends are the various behaviours, attitudes, customs, status, values, groupings, etc. of people as social animals. They are important to managers because the way people are organised and behave is relevant to the organisation's products and services. For example, if you intend to introduce a product in a certain area, it would be useful to get a demographic profile of the population there. You are not going to have much success selling holidays for the elderly in an area with a low percentage of people over 65.

Social trends typically cover the following areas:

◆ population (demographics)

◆ households and families

◆ education

◆ labour market

◆ income and wealth

◆ expenditure

◆ health

◆ crime and justice

◆ housing

◆ environment

◆ transport

◆ lifestyles.

The Office for National Statistics in the UK publishes an invaluable document each year on national social trends called Social Trends. *See the 'More @' section at the end of this theme for more details.*

Social trends are a key focus for market analysis as you can find out about the various attitudes, behaviours and lifestyles of your customers or potential customers.

Demographics

One area of particular interest to the market analyst is demographics. This is the study of population trends such as:

◆ population size and movement

◆ birth and death rates

◆ age, gender and ethnic origin.

How does this affect organisations? Well, consider two of these areas – age and gender – in the UK context.

Because of the baby boom in the 1950s, by 2015 or so the number of older people will outnumber the working population by a higher percentage – the 'dependency ratio'. This has obvious implications for pensions and health services and those providing them. Organisations in general may also wish to tap into the 'grey market' both for their supply of labour and as a target for their goods and services. For example, Web marketers are becoming increasingly aware of the grey market as a potential target for their products.

The increase of women in the labour market also has implications for organisations in terms of targeted marketing, family friendly policies, equal opportunities and part-timer rights (many new jobs for women are part time).

For information about demographics and differences between groups in society, check out the latest edition of British Social Attitudes. *See the 'More @' section at the end of this theme for more details.*

Social responsibility and business ethics

Society's attitudes towards organisations have put social responsibility and business ethics on the organisation's agenda. While the anti-capitalist riots in Seattle in 1999 and Prague in 2000 can be seen as extreme examples, many reputable non-government agencies worldwide have expressed concerns about the power of corporations to operate globally to their own advantage and without reference to the impact they have on the communities in which they operate. The UN Global Compact, signed in June 2000, could be seen as a reflection of this unease. It is a code of good conduct for international organisations covering human rights, workers' rights and protection of the environment.

See www.unglobalcompact.org for more information about the UN Global Compact.

Social responsibility is the attitude of organisations to their stakeholders. It has come to be associated with business ethics – the belief that you do something because it is right, whatever the economic consequences. Social responsibility is a moral obligation to act in the right way towards stakeholders, rather than a legal one. It is frequently associated with the organisation's attitudes to the eco-environment, local employment issues, ethical investment, exploitation of workers in poor countries, animal rights (we are all animals), executive bonuses, chemical-free products, and so on.

Not everyone shares this interpretation. Professor Milton Friedman, the brains behind modern monetarist policy, asserted that the only social responsibility an organisation has is towards its shareholders.

CALGARY, Alberta, Canada, April 10, 2001
Talisman Energy Inc. released its first independently verified Corporate Social Responsibility Report today. The report focuses on the company's Sudan operations and measures compliance with the International Code of Ethics for Canadian Business that Talisman adopted in December 1999.

The Corporate Social Responsibility Report was developed with the assistance of experts in business ethics and social auditing. It evaluates Talisman's progress towards achieving objectives in the areas of human rights, community participation, employee rights, ethical business conduct and health, safety and environment.

The report was independently verified by PricewaterhouseCoopers, UK, and includes stakeholder commentary gathered during the course of their work. The verification process included site visits to Khartoum, the concession area, a village along the pipeline and interviews with non-governmental organizations in Nairobi that operate in southern Sudan. PricewaterhouseCoopers also interviewed senior management, reviewed policies and processes and tested supporting evidence in the course of its review.

'We hope this report will be received as an honest effort to respond to concerns about our investment in Sudan,' said Dr. Jim Buckee, Talisman's President and Chief Executive Officer. 'In preparing this report and having it independently verified we believe we have provided an accurate and balanced picture of what we have done in terms of social responsibility and what we are trying to do in Sudan. To the best of our ability, and with the assistance of stakeholders, we will continue to address social issues in a responsible and inclusive fashion'.

Talisman is one of the first Canadian companies to formally measure social performance against an established code of conduct. The report has established a comprehensive framework from which the company can expand the reporting process in future years.

Source: *Business Wire* (2001b)

Clearly, having moral obligations can have a cost element. For example, large organisations like BP spend millions each year on charitable donations and local community schemes. Ethical investments, for example, have shown reasonable returns in recent times, but what would be the cost to drugs companies like GlaxoSmithKline if they drop their patent protection on drugs in third world countries to lower the price? They argue it takes years of research and development and plenty of money to get these drugs to the market in the first place. If they have to give them away cheaply, what is in it for them?

There is some evidence that social responsibility pays off in the long run as customers and other stakeholders regard organisations in a more favourable light and trade with them.

For more information about ethical investing, see the 'More @' section at the end of this theme.

Activity 14
Social trends

Objective

This activity will help you to consider the impact of social trends on organisations. It asks you to explore a demographic profile and assess its implications for organisations.

Social trends are the various behaviours, attitudes, customs, status, values, groupings etc. of people as social animals. In this activity you will look specifically at demographics.

Demographics is the study of population trends such as population size, population movement, birth and death rates, age, gender and ethnic origin. It is useful for organisations in that it can provide details of your customer base.

Task

1 Read the gay profile below.

2 Make a five or six-point list of what you think the implications are for organisations which wish to tap the gay market – what actions should they take to develop the market.

The gay profile

- 77% of gay men and lesbians are ABC1s, i.e. top socio-economic groups

- 27% have college/university education compared with 9% of general population

- 90% have no dependants

- 40% of gay men and lesbians earn over £25,000 compared with 25% for the UK as a whole

- employment levels and pension ownership are higher than national average

- 90% eat out regularly

- 79% take two or more holidays a year

- 35% visit a gay pub or club every week

- 65% will boycott companies with gay-unfriendly policies

- Brighton and London are the gay hotspots for US tourists

- Gay Pride festival now attracts 250,000 people.

Source: *Fry* (1997)

Actions organisations could take:

Feedback

Here are some possible actions for organisations wishing to tap the gay market:

1 Develop a demographic profile of your gay customers.

2 Advertise in gay magazines like *Gay Times*.

3 Develop equal opportunities policies that include sexual orientation, HIV and AIDS.

4 Develop a business presence at gay festivals, fairs and exhibitions.

5 Encourage gay recruitment.

6 Target specific geographical gay areas like Brighton and London.

7 Target the holiday, pension, entertainment and leisure market (as appropriate).

8 Sponsor gay events – Virgin has backed various Pride events.

The macro environment: technology

> 'Technology...the knack of so arranging the world that we need not experience it.'
>
> **Max Frisch (1911–1991)**

The influence of technology on the organisation is tremendous. Technology has moved civilisation from straw hats and oxen to virtual reality and high-speed trains, and from 100 beads on an abacus to sixty-gigabyte PCs. Suddenly, everything seems solvable. Yet people still get diseases and die, workers still work, organisations go bust and stocks still plummet. So what's new?

What's new?

What's new is Dean Kamen's 'Ginger'

American inventor Dean Kamen has a new invention. It's called 'Ginger'. He recently invented one called iBot. This is a wheelchair that goes up stairs. It's even been to the top of the Eiffel Tower. But back to Ginger. Ginger is an energy-related product. It's the next big thing. Harvard Business School Press have agreed to pay a Connecticut writer, Steve Kemper, $250,000 to write a book about it. It's pollution related. It's water related. It's, it's... That's the problem, Kamen won't say exactly what it is. Ginger is a mystery. Someone has suggested it's a new kind of motorised scooter running on a small, super-efficient Stirling engine with a world-changing power source. But, nobody can be sure. Ginger is a mystery.

Source: *Adapted from The Sunday Telegraph Magazine* (2001)

For organisations, technology is about labour-saving devices, increased productivity, new ways of working and smarter, quicker, more efficient systems and processes.

In modern times it is about:

- information technology (IT) – PCs, hand-helds, intranets, extranets, the Internet
- digital electronics – broadbanding, digital TV, mobiles (WAP and 3G)
- new synthetic materials – synthetic drugs, celluloid, polymers
- new energy sources – wind power, solar power, wave power, fuel-cell technology
- micro-technologies – fibre optics, microchips
- biotechnology – cloning, genetically modified foods, human genome mapping.

To find out more about new technologies, try the site www.globaltechnoscan.com/archive.htm

Good or bad?

From the organisational point of view, as from a general point of view, new technology has its good and bad points, as Table 4.2 illustrates. Which you choose to emphasise depends on your point of view.

Good points about new technology	Bad points about new technology
◆ Creates new and more interesting jobs	◆ Creates unemployment and dehumanises work
◆ Makes work environments healthy	◆ Creates new dangers for employees, e.g. Seveso, Chernobyl, Bhopal
◆ Develops new products	◆ Creates pollution
◆ Revolutionises communications	◆ You are always on call; employees are always on the Internet
◆ Increases productivity and profits	◆ Costs a lot to implement; does not work; is out of date quickly

Table 4.2 *Good and bad in new technology*

Think about how technology has impacted on your organisation – for good or bad? What have been the implications?

Information technology (IT)

A particular application of new technology which is most relevant to organisations is IT. In fact, it is more than just an application; it can be a strategic choice. IT impacts on all your activities:

◆ You use IT for administrative purposes – computerised records and reports, data processing

◆ You use IT to communicate – for example, Internet, intranet, e-mail, mobile phone, voice mail, video-conferencing

◆ You use IT for computer-based analyses for decision making, and for monitoring and control activities, for example software for business awareness analyses such as SWOT, benchmarking, balanced scorecard, etc.

◆ You use IT to produce goods – computer-controlled production processes, design processes such as CAD (computer-aided design)

◆ You use IT for supply, storage and distribution – for example electronic point of sale (EPOS), electronic data interchange (EDI), extranets.

The Internet and its technologies are an enduring source of argument in business today. Some set up e-commerce sites which nobody looks at, or whose costs exceed expectations, or which never expect to make a profit; others are having runaway success and point to the low cost base once the site is set up. The technology itself is a source of heated debate. It is too slow,

> making complex interactions difficult, yet broadbanding is becoming available, but rather more slowly than anticipated. WAP phones were all the rage, yet they are not quite up to the job. A text-based Web page on a tiny screen is not quite the same thing as the Internet experience on the computer. This may change with third generation models, which may lead to m-commerce – doing business on your always-connected mobile phone – and Bluetooth technology means using your phone to open your garage door and switch the heating on and...

What are the costs and benefits of new technology for your organisation?

Activity 15
The impact of technology

Objectives

This activity concerns the impact of technology on organisations and is based on a case study. Use it to:

◆ examine the impact of technology on the organisation

◆ assess how to deal with the introduction of new technology.

Case study

Read the case study/survey before you complete the task.

> **The Impact of Digital Technology on Small Businesses in the Media Industry**
>
> The television industry in the UK is changing rapidly. Deregulation, the introduction of new technology and new channels will have serious consequences for the future. Digital technology in particular will transform television production and broadcasting. This paper analyses the effect of digital technology on small businesses in the Welsh television industry. Wales was chosen as a case study as it has a vibrant small business sector producing television programmes.
>
> The majority of the companies in the survey were very small: 77 per cent employed less than 10 people; 91 per cent employed less than 20 people; 6 per cent employed between 21 and 30 people; and only 3 per cent employed 31 or more people. The majority of the firms had a turnover of less than £2 million: 49 per cent of the

companies had a turnover of less than £0.5 million; 68 per cent had a turnover of less than £1 million; 22 per cent had a turnover of between £1 and £2 million; and 10 per cent had a turnover in excess of £2 million.

Although a large proportion of the firms intended to produce programmes for digital television, there appeared to be some uncertainty, with 59 per cent of the production companies and 35 per cent of the supply companies being unsure or disagreeing with the statement that digitalisation was likely to provide more opportunities for them. Although the additional broadcasting hours for digital television means that there will be increased opportunities in the long term, many of the respondents were uncertain about the short term. One of the problems is the perception that only the larger firms will be able to achieve the economies of scale required for digital programme making.

Although 52 per cent agreed or agreed strongly with the statement that digitalisation would open up new markets for them, only 40 per cent of the supply companies expressed the same level of optimism. It is possible that the supplier companies are less certain of their future as a result of digitalisation as the emphasis on cost may lead companies to vertically integrate and provide the production facilities usually provided by the freelancers and facilities companies for themselves in-house. A few companies have already decided on this course of action.

Keeping up to date with technological advances in the field of digital television must be a daunting task for a small business owner/manager in the Welsh media industry, especially given the fact that they are unlikely to have had a technical education. This lack of training in the technological advances in the field is likely to increase the uncertainty. S4C held seminars in order to inform the independent television producers about digitalisation but 56 per cent agreed or strongly agreed that more training is needed.

Of the television production companies surveyed, 55 per cent were unsure about whether digital television was a good idea, indicating that there is a lot of uncertainty concerning digital television. One interviewee said that the main problem with digitalisation was that many of the smaller companies did not understand digitalisation. Some of those responses indicated that digital television was not the way forward and other technological advances would overtake digital technology. Some of the problems mentioned were that it is necessary to buy a separate decoder and that geographically remote parts of the country, including large parts of Wales, will not be able to receive digital programmes. These problems have been largely overcome with the supply of free decoders. Nevertheless, these concerns reflect the fact that it is difficult, particularly for smaller firms, to keep up with developments and many of them prefer to wait until something is proven before they make an investment.

There was a certain amount of cynicism on the part of the small business owners/managers and many felt that new technological developments were being used by large customers and suppliers to save costs, usually at their expense. Large customers and suppliers can insist that smaller companies comply with their requirements and this can lead to resentment.

The smaller companies in this study felt especially vulnerable to changes in technology, particularly those which were imposed on them. Some were uncertain about their future and felt that cost savings were being introduced under the guise of technological changes. The pressure of digital television may encourage larger companies and may force the smaller companies out of business or to join forces with larger companies.

There was a difference in attitudes towards digital television among the owners/managers interviewed. Some were enthusiastic and looked for new opportunities such as the development of new technology, including virtual reality, new channel opportunities, etc. The small businesses which embrace the changing technology and adapt their businesses to the requirements of the new technology are more likely to survive and grow.

Source: *Adapted from Fuller-Love* (2000)

Task

1 Make a list of points on how the introduction of digitalisation might impact – for better or worse – on small businesses in the media industry.

Impact of digitalisation:

2 What are the implications for small businesses in the industry –
   what must they do in the face of digitalisation?

Implications for small businesses:

Feedback

1 **Possible impacts of digitalisation on small businesses in the media industry are:**

   ◆ difficulties in achieving economies of scale for digital programme making

   ◆ digitalisation will open up markets for programme makers but not necessarily for suppliers

   ◆ lack of understanding of the new technology

   ◆ uncertainty about its staying power and suitability for Wales

   ◆ pressure to merge with larger companies as part of a cost-cutting exercise

   ◆ new opportunities provided by developments such as virtual reality, new channels.

2 **The implications could include:**

   ◆ adapt or be adapted

   ◆ get training in the new technology

   ◆ take advantage of the new opportunities, extra channels and extra hours.

The macro environment: legislation

Legislation is the fifth of the external environment factors which impact on organisations. Obviously it links with political factors as well. The idea here is to look at the impacts of legislation on organisations from three different angles, affecting three different stakeholders: employment law (employees), consumer law (customers) and corporate law (owners).

Employment law

Employment law is a good example of political factors and social factors interlinking, and this has an economic impact in terms of the costs and benefits of employment law for the organisation.

Table 4.3 gives a brief explanation of some of the key UK laws affecting employment.

Employment laws	What they cover
Health and Safety at Work Act 1974	Employer has to ensure the health, safety and welfare at work of all its employees and third parties
Sex Discrimination Act 1975 & Race Relations Act 1976	Employers must not discriminate against employees in recruitment, selection, terms and conditions, training, promotion, transfer and dismissal on sex or race grounds
Trade Union and Labour Relations Consolidation Act 1992 (as amended by Employment Relations Act 1999)	◆ Employees have the right to belong, or not belong, to a trade union and the right not to be discriminated against as a result ◆ Strike ballots must be held before strike action ◆ Trade unions have a conditional right to recognition
Disability Discrimination Act 1995	◆ Employers with 20 or more employees must not discriminate against disabled persons in recruitment, promotion, terms of employment, transfer, training, working conditions and dismissal ◆ Employers must make reasonable adjustments to the workplace or working conditions to avoid disadvantage to a disabled employee
Employment Rights Act 1996 (as amended by Employment Relations Act 1999)	◆ Employees cannot be unfairly dismissed if they have one year's continuous service ◆ Employees have a right to written particulars of their contract of employment ◆ Pregnant women have a right to maternity leave and right to return; there is also a right to paternity leave, and a right to time off for domestic incidents
Data Protection Act 1998	◆ Manually-held personal data and computer-held data must be obtained, used, processed, etc. lawfully and fairly, and must generally be available for scrutiny by the individual ◆ Sensitive data, that is data relating to racial and ethnic origin, trade union membership, sexual life, medical health, political opinions, religious beliefs and criminal convictions, can only be processed for employment purposes if permitted by law
Employment Relations Act 1999	◆ Employees have the right to be accompanied by a fellow employee or trade union representative of their choice in disciplinary and grievance procedures ◆ Part-time employees have the same rights as full-time workers regarding pay, benefits, pensions, etc.

Table 4.3 *Key UK employment laws*

The Human Rights Act 1998 also has employment rights implications regarding:

◆ Respect for private and family life – Can you spy on employees' e-mails or tap their telephone conversations? Is there a right to a proper work/family balance?

◆ Freedom of thought, conscience and religion – Can you refuse employees time off for religious festivals?

◆ Freedom of expression – Can you tell people what to wear or how long their hair should be?

◆ Freedom of peaceful assembly and association with others – Can peaceful picketing be limited to six people? Does the law of trespass infringe the right to peaceful assembly?

Such issues will be decided by the courts in the years to come.

How could the Human Rights Act – and employment laws – affect your organisation in terms of employee relations, costs of compliance and costs of non-compliance?

Consumer law

From the point of view of the customer, consumer protection law is a very good thing. Most organisations would agree as they would like to be known for quality products.

Table 4.4 gives a brief explanation of some of the key laws in this area.

Consumer protection laws	What they cover
Trade Descriptions Act 1968	It is illegal to make a false or misleading description of goods, or a false statement or description of prices
Sale of Goods Act 1979	Goods must match their description, be of satisfactory quality, and be fit for the purpose for which they are intended
Consumer Protection Act 1987	Goods must follow a 'general safety requirement' relating to manufactured goods based on UK/EU standards

Table 4.4 *Key consumer laws*

Corporate law

By corporate law, we mean law that attempts to regulate business practice or organisation, such as company law and competition law. The stakeholders most affected here are business owners, though competition law clearly also affects consumers.

Byers intervenes in TV deals

Stephen Byers, Secretary of State for Trade and Industry, stunned the City when he referred two of Britain's biggest recent media deals, both involving French companies, to the Competition Commission.

The deals under scrutiny are Vivendi's increased holding in BSkyB, the satellite broadcaster, and the £8.2 billion acquisition of CWC, the cable television company, by America's NTL. The CWC deal was partly financed by France Telecom, which injected £3.4 billion into NTL in return for a 25 per cent stake in the company, which it can increase to 34 per cent after 2002. Vivendi, headed by Jean Marie-Messier, is a vast conglomerate whose interests range from water utilities to telecoms and media. France Telecom, meanwhile, is one of the country's largest communications groups.

The shock in the City was compounded by the fact that Mr Byers ignored the advice of the Office of Fair Trading (OFT) by referring the CWC deal to the Commission. The Trade Secretary decided that the acquisition of CWC's residential cable interests 'raised sufficient concerns' over the pay-television market to justify a referral. Barclay Knapp, chief executive of NTL, found out about the decision while reporting third-quarter results to Wall Street. NTL sources said he was shocked into silence when he heard the news.

The referral appears to go against the thinking of regulatory bodies such as the Independent Television Commission, which have previously suggested that further consolidation in the cable industry would help to promote more effective competition for BSkyB, which is 40 per cent owned by News International, owner of *The Times*.

Cable companies do not compete with each other anyway, because they operate in regional franchise areas.

Mr Byers's decision to refer Vivendi's 24.7 per cent stake in BSkyB caused even greater surprise. Vivendi, which has a controlling stake in the French television company Canal Plus, originally acquired a 17 per cent stake in BSkyB from Pathé, the French film company. Vivendi then bought a further 7.5 per cent stake in BSkyB from Granada and Pearson, the UK media groups.

The initial deals with Granada and Pearson were dependent on regulatory approval, but when the deals were finalised in the last couple of months they became unconditional. Mr Byers said the Vivendi acquisition raised concern about 'the market for film and sports rights and for conditional access technology in the UK'.

Source: *The Times* (1999)

Table 4.5 gives a brief explanation of some of the laws in this area.

Corporate laws	What they cover
The Companies Acts 1948 and 1985	◆ Every company must have a memorandum of association, a set of articles of association, and a register of members ◆ Companies must have their accounts audited by registered auditors and must submit annual reports and accounts to the Registrar of Companies within certain time limits
Fair Trading Act 1973	The Competition Commission can investigate monopolies in the supply of goods and services, or the export of goods, covering 25% of the market or more, and mergers where the merger creates a group with 25% or more of the market, or adds market share to such a monopoly, or the acquired assets are valued at £15 million or more
Competition Act 1998	◆ Prohibition of agreements and practices which prevent, restrict or distort competition, or are intended to do so, and which may affect trade within the UK ◆ Prohibition of abuse by companies of a dominant position in a market which may affect trade within the UK
Regulation of Investigatory Powers Act 2000	Gives the government powers to initiate surveillance of company websites and take possession of encryption keys

Table 4.5 *Key corporate laws*

Not all law is legislation

It is worth pointing out that not all law is legislation – at least as far as the UK goes. Common law – law historically made by judges rather than legislative bodies such as Parliament – may also impact on organisations. The law relating to negligence, for example, is common law. Consider the impact of judgements in the area of health and safety regarding repetitive strain injury (RSI), passive smoking and stress. These were based on the law of negligence (duty of care), not the Health and Safety at Work Act.

For more information about the laws in this section and other relevant laws, see the 'More @' section at the end of this theme.

Activity 16
Legislation

Objectives

This activity will help you to:

◆ examine the impact of legislation on organisations

◆ assess the organisation's reactions to legislation.

In this activity we will focus on employment law.

Task

1 Consider the Employment Relations Act 1999. You can find out about this law by searching on the Internet.

2 Explain what the law means organisations, such as your own, have to do which they didn't do before.

3 What are the time, cost, administrative and organisational implications of the law?

What organisations must do	Implications

Feedback

2 The Employment Relations Act 1999 means you have to:

♦ discuss recognition rights with trade unions and accept trade unions for collective bargaining if the workforce votes in favour

♦ alter your maternity leave policy again

♦ develop a new policy on paternity leave, and a policy on the right to time off for domestic incidents

♦ alter your disciplinary and grievance procedures to include an employee's right to be accompanied by a fellow employee or trade union representative of their choice at hearings

♦ give part-time employees the same rights as full-time workers regarding pay, benefits, pensions etc.

3 The implications are new costs to allow for new leave entitlements, a new way of handling industrial relations, extra costs per part-time workers, reorganisation of administration for part-time workers' pay, benefits etc., and the time and costs involved when drawing up new policy documentation.

The macro environment: eco-enviromental factors

The eco-environment is now a key topic of global, EU, national and local debate. It is not just a social responsibility issue either; there could be profitability impacts for organisations not listening to Mother Nature.

What's the problem?

There are a number of concerns regarding the impact of the eco-environment on businesses which are closely associated with the way businesses have impacted on the eco-environment:

- Global warming – carbon dioxide and other greenhouse gases may create climatic changes which flood businesses out, put up their insurance premiums or destroy their crops.

- Pollution – consider how oil spills affect the fishing industry and tourism.

- Unsustainable development – can cut down your resource base which puts up costs.

- Farming methodology – consider the impact of the foot-and-mouth outbreak in the UK (2001). Costs to the industry and other affected industries are estimated in the region of at least £9 billion.

- Nuclear power – how many businesses are flourishing around Chernobyl?

A problem for business

The idea that businesses are not concerned with a 'soft' issue like the eco-environment is not the case. Many are now well aware of possible impacts of the eco-environment on their businesses, and are looking for solutions, particularly in the US. The chemical industry in the following example is a case in point.

As you read it, notice how political, technological, eco-environmental and social factors all become involved. The political aspect is the 160 countries looking for an agreement under the Kyoto Protocol. The technological aspect is the belief that new technology can reduce the rate of climate change – fuel-cell technology, for example. The eco-environmental aspect is the issue of global warming and climate change, and the social aspect is the effect of climate change on the peoples of the world.

Chemical Industry Seeks New Tech Approach to Combat Global Warming

An industry coalition representing chemical manufacturers and other US business groups says the failure of negotiators to reach agreement on implementing the Kyoto Protocol signals the need for a new approach to address concerns about global warming.

'These negotiations led us down a dead-end street,' says Glenn Kelly, executive director of the Global Climate Coalition, whose membership includes the American Chemistry Council.

'The time has come for a new direction on climate policy based on the ability of businesses to lead the development of new technologies to address global concerns about greenhouse gas emissions,' Mr. Kelly declares.

Two weeks of negotiations among 160 countries closed November 25 in The Hague without agreement on measures to fight global warming, after the US and the European Union failed to settle a bitter dispute over ways to cut greenhouse gas emissions implicated in climate change.

Mr. Kelly says the outcome of the UN-sponsored talks marks a complete collapse of efforts to set the specific rules for implementing the 1997 Kyoto treaty among nations of the world.

'American businesses looking for the rules of the road under the Kyoto Protocol have been left high and dry,' he says.

Mr. Kelly says any eventual climate agreement under the protocol would have to include credits for forests and farmlands that absorb carbon dioxide, a workable system for buying, selling and trading emissions credits and a rational mechanism that encourages unlimited transfers of technology to developing nations.

Source: *Chemical Market Reporter* (2000)

It is worth noting that many businesses have adopted international standards on the environment – the quality-based ISO 14000 series.

If you don't listen to Mother Nature...

...then there are others out there to make you listen. Stakeholders seem to be abundant when it comes to the eco-environment, and it is not just direct action groups. Buyers may cancel the contracts of their suppliers if they do not behave in a socially responsible and eco-environmentally friendly way.

Royal Dutch/Shell cancelled 106 such agreements in 2001 alone. Pension funds can put pressure on as shareholders – Pirc, the pensions consultancy, following a campaign by Greenpeace, wanted

4 The macro environment

BP Amoco to reveal its strategy for managing the business risks relating to climate change (2001). Local people can hold up planning applications for quarries. If, in the end, you do not do something voluntarily, legislation can impact on you – for example the Environmental Protection Act 1990 and landfill tax.

Activity 17
An eco-environmental audit

Objective

In this activity you are going to find out about the eco-environment affecting your organisation. It will help you to carry out an eco-environmental audit of your organisation/area of work and make suggestions for change.

Task

1 Use the chart below to complete a brief eco-environmental audit of your organisation/area of work. The 'specifics' give you some ideas of what to look out for.

Areas to cover	Specifics	Comments
Energy	Lights, machinery left on Heating left on, too hot Badly maintained machines and equipment Energy-wasting machines	
Water	Leaking water Boiling too much water Water rates	
Waste	Reuse and recycle practices Cost of waste disposal	
Noise	Poorly maintained machines and equipment Personal protective equipment	
Air	Adequate indoor ventilation Air conditioning	

Areas to cover	Specifics	Comments
Transport	Policy on travelling to work Company car policy (e.g. green fuel)	
Awareness	Are staff aware of wasting energy/water etc.? Is there an environmental policy and if so, is it any good? Is there a system for environmental complaints from the public?	

2 Make some suggestions for improvements.

Suggestions:

Feedback

Discuss your findings with work colleagues. Do colleagues agree with your suggestions for improvements? What would you need to do to implement your suggestions?

The readiness of colleagues to help with implementation may depend on how far your organisation and your colleagues recognise eco-environmental factors as an important issue for them.

PESTLE analysis

The macro environment can be analysed using a technique known as PESTLE analysis. PESTLE stands for political, economic, social, technological, legislative/legal, eco-environmental. Sometimes it is shortened to PEST, with the legislative/legal factors bundled with the political ones and the eco-environmental with the social.

The PESTLE factors

The PESTLE analysis aims to make a list of all the macro-environmental factors impacting on your organisation. Table 4.6 summarises what you might be looking for.

You can use a similar table to this when undertaking your PESTLE analysis.

Political

- Local, national, EU, global policies
- Administrative burden
- Tax, tax, tax
- Political influence/pressure – lobbying

Economic

- Inflation, unemployment, trade
- GDP, consumption, investment, growth
- Deregulation
- Monetary policy (interest rates), fiscal policy
- Globalisation

Social

- Demographics (national and local) – age, gender, race
- Households, education, health
- Income distribution, expenditure
- Lifestyles and work/leisure balance
- Social responsibility and business ethics

Technological

- Information technology (IT), digital electronics
- New synthetic materials
- New energy sources
- Micro-technologies
- Biotechnology
- Costs/benefits, implementation, obsolescence

Legislative/legal

- Employment law – health, data protection, race, sex, disability, employment rights, employment relations
- Consumer law – description of goods, sale of goods, safety of goods
- Corporate law – company law, fair trading, competition law, surveillance

Eco-environmental

- Global warming (energy consumption)
- Pollution
- Unsustainable development
- Methodologies and processes – farming, nuclear power
- Stakeholder power/influence

Table 4.6 *PESTLE factors*

> **An example**
> Imagine you wish to develop a new Internet-linked GSM (Global System for Mobile communications) mobile phone which provides just data rather than being voice enabled, for example figures and statistics for field vulcanologists. What might you want to ask yourself from a PESTLE point of view? See Table 4.7.

Of course, a full analysis would go beyond these basic questions, explore them and produce hard evidence. But PESTLE will give you the criteria you need to consider.

Political	*Economic*
◆ Are the politicians in the UK and EU creating a favourable climate for mobile phone technology?	◆ What about the downturn in the TMT (technology, media and telecommunications) market?
◆ What about escalating licence fees?	◆ Is EU R&D funding available for specific applications?

Social	*Technological*
◆ Would it be a 'smart' thing to have?	◆ Isn't GSM too slow?
◆ Will this gadget catch on with the young who like text-based communications?	◆ Will the technology be outflanked by new technology?
◆ Will it appeal to all tastes?	◆ Is the 'push' technology it utilises a positive or negative factor?
◆ Is it a leisure device or a work device, or both?	

Legislative/legal	*Eco-environmental*
◆ Does it conform to health and safety regulations?	◆ What about mobile phone aerial masts – isn't there a looming problem about them?
◆ What about its 'always on' feature when used in a car? Is it a distraction?	

Table 4.7 *Example of PESTLE factors at work*

How is PESTLE used?

The way you use a PESTLE analysis depends on what you carried it out for in the first place. Usually, and dependent on any other analyses, you can use it to inform your strategy development and your planning. It could be used for a marketing strategy, for a financial, corporate, developmental, project or operational strategy, or all of these things together.

To find examples of PESTLE analyses, search the Internet using the key words 'PESTLE'/'PEST' or 'PESTLE analysis', or ask around your organisation to see if there are previous ones around.

Activity 18
PESTLE analysis

Objective

PESTLE analysis is the quintessential analysis tool for assessing factors in the external environment. This activity asks you to carry out a PESTLE analysis on your organisation.

Task

1   Use the chart below to list the key trends and forces in the macro environment that will affect your organisation.

Political	*Economic*

Social	*Technological*

Legislative/legal	*Eco-environmental*

2   What might your organisation need to do in the face of these opportunities/threats?

What needs to be done:

Feedback

Have a look at back at the text to check if you have correctly covered the main areas of the PESTLE analysis. Discuss your analysis with colleagues. Have they identified similar factors? You may want to consider what impact these factors are likely to have on the organisation.

◆ Recap

This theme has looked at all the external factors that are likely to impact on the operation and success of an organisation.

Evaluate the impact of political factors on organisations

◆ The range of political factors impacting on organisations is wide, including taxation, local and national government policies, EU and global politics.

Define some key economic terms and assess the impact of European Monetary Union on your organisation

◆ This section looks at macro-economic concepts such as GDP, consumption, savings and investments, national debt, inflation, trade gaps, growth rates, monetary policy, fiscal policy and how they impact on you in your organisation.

◆ EMU is likely to have an effect on your organisation – here you look at the impact in terms of pros and cons.

Examine social trends and explore a demographic profile to assess its implications for organisations

◆ Social trends are the various behaviours, attitudes, customs, status, values, groupings of people in society.

◆ Demographics is the study of social trends, including population size and movement, birth and death rates, age and gender.

◆ To illustrate the effects of social trends you explore the implications of the gay profile for your organisation.

Consider the organisational impact of new technologies

◆ For organisations, technology is about labour-saving devices, increased productivity, new ways of working and smarter, quicker, more efficient systems and processes.

◆ Is new technology always good for an organisation? Here you examine the costs and benefits of new technology.

See how three types of legislation impact on three different stakeholders: employment law (employees), consumer law (customers) and corporate law (owners)

- Employment law is a good example of legislation impacting on an organisation and directly impacting on the way you manage. It affects health and safety, discrimination, labour relations, employment rights, data protection and employment relations.

- Consumer law covers key areas such as trade descriptions, sale of goods and consumer protection.

- Corporate law covers setting up companies, fair trading, competition, investigatory powers.

Carry out an eco-environmental audit of your organisation or work area

- Changes in the environment due to pollution are now a problem for all businesses and organisations.

- It is not uncommon for an organisation to lose a contract on the basis of its attitude to environmental issues.

- There are a number of areas in which you, as a manager, can have an impact, including energy and water conservation, dealing with waste, noise reduction, air pollution, transport issues and employee awareness.

Carry out a PESTLE analysis

- PESTLE analysis brings together a review of the political, economic, social, technological, legal and eco-environmental factors impacting on organisations.

- A PESTLE analysis can be used for informing marketing strategy and financial, corporate, developmental, project or operational strategy.

 **More @**

Bailey, J. (1993) *Managing People and Technological Change,* **FT Prentice Hall**
This is a good book to read for the people management implications of technology. It explores the impact of new technology on people and their jobs and how, through the use of job design and work organisational concepts, it is possible to achieve a match between human and technological needs.

Campbell, D., Stonehouse, G. and Houston, B. (2002) 2nd edition, *Business Strategy: an Introduction*, Elsevier Butterworth-Heinemann
This is an accessible textbook that provides a straightforward and comprehensive guide to complex issues and concepts. See Chapters 6 'Analysis of the macroenvironment' and Chapter 8 'Competitive advantage: strategies, knowledge and core competences'.

***British Social Attitudes: the 17th Report: Focusing on Diversity* (2000), Sage Publications Ltd**
www.sagepub.com/series.aspx?sid=30&sc=2
For more about demographics and differences between groups in society, check out the diversity edition of *British Social Attitudes*. Most of the chapters examine the extent to which various sub-groups in society differ from one another in their attitudes, values and perspectives. The topics are generational differences, health care rationing, the working class and New Labour, sex and the media, gender differences, loss of faith, images of council housing, national identity after devolution, town and country life, and begging.

Leglisation

For more details of the laws in this theme and other relevant laws, you could check out Her Majesty's Stationery Office at **www.legislation.hmso.gov.uk**. See Directgov at **www.open.gov.uk/hse** for health and safety law, **www.dataprotection.gov.uk** (Office of the Information Commissioner), **www.tradingstandards.net**, a private 'not for profit' advice resource for consumer law, **www.oft.gov.uk** (Office of Fair Trading) for competition and fair trading law.

EMU – **http://europa.eu.int/comm/economy_finance/euro/benefits/benefits_main_en.htm**
This website presents the case for European Monetary Union. It is the website of the European Union and outlines the macroeconomic framework.

Organisations and the environmental challenge

Carry out some research on the Internet to find out about these key elements of the macro environment: EU treaties; G7/G8 treaties; new technologies that are relevant and important to your industry; the business response to environmental challenges via the World Business Council for Sustainable Development website, **www.wbcsd.ch**

The Office for National Statistics

The Office for National Statistics in the UK publishes an invaluable document each year on national social trends called *Social Trends*. It contains information on a range of social policy areas, described in tables, charts and with explanatory text. You can download a free copy of the latest edition from **www.statistics.gov.uk/products/p5443.asp**

Full references are provided at the end of the book.

5

SWOT analysis

What are the implications of macro-environmental factors on your organisation? Read about an analysis tool that brings together the internal and external factors that impact on an organisation.

You will be asked to summarise the key internal and external factors that are important to your organisation, looking at factors such as:

◆ What are your organisation's distinctive competencies?

◆ What differentiates your organisation from the competition?

◆ Which of these factors are the most important?

You will discover how the data from your SWOT analysis can drive strategy to:

◆ leverage the organisation's strengths to exploit opportunities and offset threats

◆ minimise its weaknesses to protect opportunities and offset threats.

The internal and external environment: SWOT analysis

SWOT stands for:

Strengths
Weaknesses
Opportunities
Threats

A SWOT analysis should enable you to make strategic decisions by considering:

◆ **internal** strengths and weaknesses

◆ **external** opportunities and threats.

If you know what your strengths and weaknesses are, you can decide how best to adapt to changes in the external environment.

How does SWOT work?

1 Analyse your organisation internally. Write down its strengths and weaknesses in terms of the following factors:

◆ Strategy – is it in the right direction now? Check mission and objectives, if any. What about planning?

- ◆ Culture and structure – flexibility, customer driven, team oriented, etc.

- ◆ Products and services – brand, reputation.

- ◆ People and their skills – human resources, knowledge, learning.

- ◆ Finance – debt structure, budgets, cash flow, source of income.

- ◆ Resources – land, buildings, systems, processes.

2 Analyse your department externally. Write down its opportunities and threats in terms of:

- ◆ The industry and marketplace in which it operates. You could draw on a Porter's Five Forces analysis to do this or on market research into your customer base.

- ◆ Trends in the macro environment, using a PESTLE analysis to highlight important political, economic, social, technological, legislative and eco-environmental trends that are affecting your organisation now and will affect it in the future.

3 Assess how you can create a strategy based on:

- ◆ utilising strengths

- ◆ minimising weaknesses

- ◆ taking opportunities

- ◆ warding off threats.

Strengths	Weaknesses
◆ Good name for innovation	◆ Financing may be a problem due to weakness of market
◆ Good sales of current products	
◆ High-quality production processes and team	◆ Lack of interest from venture capitalists
◆ Low current debt and growing operating profit	◆ Lack of clear strategy – are we in the mobile phone business or data communications business?
◆ Fairly unique product	◆ Weak marketing department
Opportunities	**Threats**
◆ Takeover of French rival on the cards	◆ New technology may outflank it
◆ Utilities showing interest for their field teams	◆ Market for mobile phone technology is fairly saturated
◆ Development of vehicle tracking service using GPS (Global Positioning System) technology could be useful spin-off	◆ Possible new health and safety regulations
	◆ BT showing interest in the market

Table 5.1 *Example of a SWOT analysis*

SWOT is a very flexible tool and can actually be applied at a number of different levels: organisational, departmental, product, operational, project and even individual. Consider the example of the mobile phone company you looked at in the previous theme, summarised in Table 4.7. From the PESTLE analysis, you already know something about the opportunities and threats. A possible SWOT analysis for this company is provided in Table 5.1.

As with PESTLE, you would have to go into the ins and outs of some of the points in the SWOT analysis in a bit more detail before you came up with any sort of strategy. A matrix based on utilising strengths, minimising weaknesses, taking opportunities and warding off threats would be useful.

Activity 19
SWOT analysis

Objectives

This activity is the key environmental activity that sums up your understanding of all the internal and external factors which impact on organisations. Use it to:

◆ conduct a SWOT analysis of your organisation/work area

◆ identify your strategic needs.

Task

1 Carry out a SWOT analysis of your organisation/work area using the chart below. Use the information from the PESTLE analysis you carried out in Activity 18 to help you, as appropriate.

2 What are the implications of your SWOT analysis in terms of strategic change, actions, plans etc.?

Strengths	Weaknesses

Opportunities	Threats

Feedback

Review this theme to check if you have correctly covered the main areas of the SWOT analysis. Discuss your ideas with your colleagues.

◆ Recap

This theme brings together the internal and external factors which impact on your organisation and proposes an analysis tool to find out your strategic strengths and needs.

Examine the key internal and external factors that are important to your organisation

◆ A SWOT analysis can be used to leverage the organisation's strengths to exploit opportunities and to offset threats and to minimise its weaknesses to protect opportunities and offset threats.

▶▶ More @

Campbell, D., Stonehouse, G. and Houston, B. (2002) 2nd edition, *Business Strategy: an Introduction*, Elsevier Butterworth-Heinemann
This is an accessible textbook that provides a straightforward and comprehensive guide to complex issues and concepts. See Chapter 4 for 'Financial analysis and performance indicators' and Chapter 5 'Products and markets' including market segmentation, product life cycles and new product development. See Chapter 6 for a new view on SWOT and PESTLE analysis – SPENT analysis.

References

Ansoff, I. (1966) *Corporate Strategy*, McGraw-Hill

Ayers, C. and Shoddy, R. (1999) 'Byers intervenes in TV deals', *The Times,* News International, 13 November

Balanced Scorecard Institute – www.balancedscorecard.org

Baron, A. and Collard, R. (1999) 'Realising our Assets', *People Management*, CIPD, 14 October, 38–45

Bogan, C. E. and English, M. J. (1994) *Benchmarking for Best Practices: Winning Through Innovative Adaptation*, McGraw-Hill

Boston Consulting Group (1977) 'Long Range Planning', *Elsevier Science Ltd,* February, 12

BP, www.bp.com

Business Wire (2000) 'Fortune Brands Exploring Strategic Options for Its Office Products Business', 9 October, 2265

Business Wire (2001a) 'Phillip Townsend Associates Predicts Dramatic Changes in the Thermoplastics Distribution Industry', 12 February, 2063

Business Wire (2001b) 'Talisman Issues Corporate Social Responsibility Report; Independently Verified Report Sent to Shareholders', 10 April, 0323

California Energy Commission (1997) 'Appendices B & C', *Strategic Plan,* May

Cannon, T. (1994) *Corporate Responsibility, A textbook on business ethics, governance, environment: roles and responsibilities*, Pitman

Cartwright, R. I. (2001) *Mastering the Business Environment*, Palgrave

Chemical Market Reporter (2000) Schnell Publishing Company, 4 December, Vol. 258, Iss. 23, 5

Clark, A. (1999) *Organisations, Competition and the Business Environment*, FT Prentice Hall

Day, G. (1999) 'Aligning Organizational Structure to the Market', *Business Strategy Review*, Autumn, Vol. 10, No. 3, 33–46

De Gorter, D. (2000) 'First Union's Design for Bank Insurance Success', *National Underwriter Life & Health – Financial Services Division,* The National Underwriter Company, 13 November, Vol. 104, Iss. 46, 8

Doz, Y. L. (1996) 'The Evolution of Co-operation in Strategic Alliances: Initial Conditions or Learning Processes?' *Strategic Management Journal*, Vol 17 (Suppl. Summer), 55–83

The Economist (2001) 'Beyond the pool; Electricity markets; Britains electricity gamble', *The Economist* (UK), 3 March, 9

Education Marketplace, www.education-net.co.uk

Exxon Mobil, www.exxon.mobil.com

Floyd, D. (2001) *International Business Environment*, FT Prentice Hall

Forster, H. (2001) 'Russian Metals Execs Mastering Politics', *American Metal Market*, Cahners Publishing Company, 5 Feb, Vol.109, Iss. 24,16

Fry, A. (1997) 'Reaching the pink pound', *Marketing,* Haymarket Publishing Ltd, 4 September, 23

Fuller-Love, N. (2000) *International Small Business Journal,* Woodcock Publications Ltd, July–September, Vol. 18, Iss. 4, 80

Global Benchmarking Council (1999) 'Sampling of Health Care Industry Web-Based Program Benefits' – www.globalbenchmarking.com

Grant, R. M. and Neupert, K. E. (1999) 2nd edition, *Contemporary Strategy Analysis*, Blackwell Publishers Ltd

Handy, C. (1993) 4th edition, *Understanding Organizations*, Penguin Books, 180–216

Harley Davidson, www.harley-davidson.com

Harvard Business School (2000) *Harvard Business Review on Business and the Environment,* Harvard Business School Press

Johnson, G. and Scholes, K. (1999) 5th edition, *Exploring Corporate Strategy*, Prentice Hall Europe

Kaplan, R. S. and Norton, D. P. (1996) *The Balanced Scorecard: Translating Strategy into Action*, Harvard Business School Press

Keynes, J. M. (1926) *The End of Laissez-Faire, pt. 1,* Irvington

Oregon State University, www.osu.orst.edu

Palmer, A., Hartley, B. and Mullholland, M. (1999) 3rd edition, *The Business and Marketing Environment*, McGraw-Hill

Peters, T. and Waterman, R. (1982) *In Search of Excellence,* Harper & Row

Pfizer, www.pfizer.com

Porter, M. E. (1980) *Competitive Strategy: Techniques for Analysing Industries and Competitors*, The Free Press

PRNewswire (2001) 'Corporate Entity Renamed Northwestern Memorial HealthCare', PRNewswire Association Inc., 18 January

Royal Dutch/Shell, www.shell.com

Singh, N. (1999), 'Organisation 2005 – P&G unveils massive culture-change exercise', *The Financial Express*, Indian Express Newspapers (Bombay), 12 October

Smith, A. (1776) *An Inquiry into the Nature and Causes of the Wealth of Nations,* full text available on the Adam Smith Institute website, www.adamsmith.org/smith

The Sunday Telegraph Magazine (2001) '21st Century Genius', 11 March

Tesco, www.tesco.com

Tichy, N. and Charan, R. (1989) 'Speed, Simplicity, and Self Confidence: An Interview with Jack Welch', *Harvard Business Review*, September/October

The Times (2000) 'Boots hopes to make strides in US with deal', News International, 18 October

The Times (2001) 'Daft' EU flowerpot ruling upheld', News International, 29 January

United Nations Global Compact, www.unglobalcompact.org

Vodafone, www.vodafone.com

Worthington, I. and Britton, C. (2000) 3rd edition, *The Business Environment*, FT Prentice Hall